POWER PLAY
Mental Toughness for Hockey and Beyond

AYNSLEY M. SMITH, RN, Ph.D.

Athletic Guide Publishing
PO Box 1050
Flagler Beach, FL 32136-1050
386.439.2250 phone
386.439.2249 fax
agp@flaglernet.com

Published by:

Athletic Guide Publishing
PO Box 1050
Flagler Beach, FL 32136-1050 USA

Copyright © 1999
Athletic Guide Publishing

3rd Edition, February 2000

ISBN 13: 978-1-60179-099-6

Dedication to the Players

This book is dedicated to competitive athletes who seek excellence in the sport of hockey. It is for those who aspire to master both the mental and physical aspects of this exhilarating, yet demanding game. It honors those who developed their skills on frozen ponds and frozen feet, often using magazines for shin-pads. Despite growing pressure on players to develop physical strength and mental toughness, it is my hope that the game never loses its players of balance, skill, and speed, for it is to them, that the game of hockey truly belongs.

AMS /91, 94, 99

ABOUT THE AUTHORS

Aynsley Smith has written "Power Play" from the perspective of a daughter, wife, mother, counselor, researcher, and fan of the hockey player. She has a Ph.D. in Kinesiology and Sport Psychology from the University of Minnesota and is an assistant professor in Orthopedic Surgery and Physical

Medicine and Rehabilitation at the Mayo Medical School. She is the sport psychology counselor and research director in the Sports Medicine Center at Mayo Clinic.

Much of Aynsley's research has been on aspects of injury to hockey players, often in collaboration with Dr. Michael Stuart. She has conducted research for several years on ice hockey goalies. She has served as the sports counselor to USHL Junior teams for many years during which time they won two National Championships and to the USA Junior National teams in 1990 - 1994, prior to their participation in the World tournaments. She has served as a sport psychology consultant to hockey teams at all levels, including the NHL, and frequently presents at USA Hockey coaching clinics, including the World Hockey Summit. Aynsley is a certified consultant in the Association for the Advancement of Applied Sport Psychology. She is shown on previous page with her husband, Hugh C. Smith, M.D.

Dr. Michael Stuart is the Co-Director of the Sports Medicine Center at Mayo Clinic. He is an associate professor in the Department of Orthopedic Surgery at the Mayo Medical

School. He has provided guidance and a valuable written contribution to Power Play. Dr. Stuart has been the team physician for a USHL Junior team for many years, served as the team physician to the USA National Select 17 team in Japan in 1991, and accompanied the United States Olympic Team on their Pre-Olympic European Tour. He has completed research on the epidemiology of injuries in Junior A hockey, which he presented at the USA Masters Coaches Symposium at the Olympic Training Center in 1992. He has published several papers on youth hockey injuries. Dr. Stuart is the principal investigator of a USA Hockey project on the relationship of head and facial protection to head and facial injuries in USHL Junior A hockey. He is a member of the USA hockey injury surveillance committee and co-chaired the Safety in Ice Hockey (ASTM) symposium in St. Louis in 1996.

Steve Finnie, M.Ed. and Tracy Fischer, B.A. collaborated on two chapters entitled "What It Means to Be a Hockey Player" and "Learning Life Skills Through Hockey". Both Steve and Tracy served as Johannson-Gund scholars in the Mayo Clinic Sports Medicine Center during 1998-1999. They assisted with applied sport psychology programs for hockey teams during the 1997-1998 and 1998-1999 season.

Other contributing authors are Kathy Krause, R.D. and Steve DeBoer, M.P.H., R.D., L.D. of the Mayo Clinic Section of Dietetics, Dave Krause, P.T., M.B.A. of the Mayo Clinic School of Physical Therapy, Lyn Gentling from Nuclear Radiology, Mayo Clinic, and Mr. John Tomberlin, P.T., Director of Sports Medicine at the Saunders Physical Therapy Institute.

Hugh M. Smith, Ph.D. and Nicole J. Detling, M.S. (ABT) served as editors of Power Play, a manual which was written for players and coaches for the sole purpose of contributing to their effectiveness and enjoyment of the game. Hugh has a degree in English and Economics, a Masters degree in Philosophy, a Ph.D. in the History of Medicine, and is now a second year medical student. Hugh was co-captain of his high school hockey team and is assistant ski patrol director at Welch Village. He is a rodeo kayaking instructor and a member of the Midwest Mountaineering Kayaking team. Nicole was a Division III three-sport athlete at Ohio Wesleyan University (basketball, indoor track and field, outdoor track and field) and is currently a Johannson-Gund scholar at the Mayo Clinic. Nicole has written three performance enhancement manuals for athletes and several bulletins for coaches which apply sport psychology principles to specific sports. Connie Bruce did the secretarial work, provided editorial assistance, and serves as business manager for the project.

ACKNOWLEDGMENTS

My thanks to coaches Jim Johannson, Mike Schwartz, Kevin Constantine, Walt Kyle, Mark Kaufman, Will Fish, Bob O'Connor, Jim Wylie, John Cunniff, Doug Woog, Bill Butters, Mark Mazzolini, Dean Blais, Mike Aikens, Kirk Gill, and Art Bergland of USA Hockey for sharing your perspectives and your teams. My appreciation to Dr. Diane Wiese-Bjornstal, Dr. Nancy Greer, Dr. Tom Moyer, Dr. B.Morrey, Dr. Ed Laskowski, Ted Drury, Jim Hiller, James Konte, and Shjon Podein for their assistance. Dave Peterson shared insights on goaltending, and Bob Frerker and the goalies attending Bob Frerker's Goalie Camp provided valuable research assistance. I also want to thank all the hockey goalies who wore heart monitors in games, provided saliva, and answered questionnaires for me. Hopefully, we are putting some of what we have learned back into the game. Some of that information from six years of research forms the basis for the **Power Play** chapter on goaltending. My Northern correspondent, Irene, in Winnipeg kept me up to date with hockey news from the Canadian side even though it was getting hard for her 92 year old eyes to see the puck. To ALL OF THE PLAYERS who have been willing to take chances, who have trusted me with their confidences and have provided feedback, it is from you and for you that we will continue to learn. Many of the wonderfully poignant quotations scattered throughout Power Play come from a small book called Sports Minded from which I have liberally borrowed. I am also indebted to Ken Johnson, the hockey guru, who exemplifies and shared a favorite quotation that apparently Badger Bob Johannson carried in his wallet:

"Keep away from people who try to belittle your ambitions. Small people always do that, but the really great make you feel that you too can become great." – Mark Twain.

Kevin Constantine
Head Coach
1997 - 1999 - Pittsburgh Penguins
1996 - Calgary Flames
1993 - 1994 - San Jose Sharks
1991 - 1993 - Kansas City Blades; HL Turner Cup Champions
1990 - 1991 - USA Junior National Team
1987 - 1988 - Rochester Mustangs; USHL National Junior Champions

"A coach must be part teacher, administrator, father, recruiter, physiologist, strategist, scholar, evaluator, motivator, and psychologist. Knowledge is essential in all these areas and with today's athlete, an understanding of sport psychology is imperative. Aynsley Smith's **Power Play** book is an invaluable tool for any coach and a practical aid for any player in developing mental toughness skills."

"I have used the material in this book with every team I've ever coached."

Walt Kyle
Head Coach
1998 - Head Coach, Hamilton, Ontario, Canada.
1994 - San Diego Gulls
1994 - Assistant Coach - USA World Cup Team
1992 - 1993 - Seattle Thunderbirds
1991 - 1992 - USA Jr. National Team, Bronze Medal Winners
1990 - 1991 - University of Northern Michigan, NCAA Champions

"Power Play is an outstanding addition to any coach's or player's library. It helps players better focus on the goals they set and it helps coaches develop their players and teams to their fullest. Without Power Play and Aynsley Smith's help, the 1992 National Junior Team (who won a bronze medal) would not have had the success it did."

"A must read for progressive dedicated hockey people."

Jim Johannson
1992 and 1988 - United States Olympic Hockey Team
Professional Player
1997 - 1998 - USHER Head Coach

"The principles and exercises in **Power Play** have benefited me both professionally and with the Olympic teams."

"Power Play will greatly enhance all players' mental preparation and development in hockey."

Mike Schwartz
Head Coach
1996 - Present - Augsburg College; MIAC Champions, 1998; Playoff Champions, 1998;
        National Coach of the Year, 1998
1992 - 1996 - Coach - White Bear Lake High School; Section Champions, 3 years;
        Section Coach of the Year
1991 - 1992 - Coach - Renon Serie B, Professional Team in Italy
1990 - 1991 - Coach - USHL Sioux City Musketeers
1986 - 1990 - Coach - St. Paul Johnson High School
1985 - 1986 - Coach - Lathrop High School; Alaska State Champions; Coach of the Year

"We used the book **Power Play** during our Final Four season here at Augsburg in the 1997-98 season and again this year!

The successes we have had can be directly attributed to the techniques used in **Power Play** and Aynsley's influence, not only on the players, but the coaches as well."

Ted Drury
1993 - Present - Professional Player
1992 - United States Olympic Hockey Team
1990 - 1991 - Captain - USA Junior National Hockey Team

"I thought Power Play was great."

Dr. Jack Blatherwick
Exercise Physiologist USA Hockey
Author of "Overspeed"

"I think **Power Play,** by Aynsley Smith, is one of the most practical books written on mental preparation for practices and games. This is not a generic book on sport psychology as it is based on a great deal of experience with hockey players and teams. There are practical examples, exercises, and diagrams that make it easy for coaches and players to learn about accepting responsibility, gaining control of our own destiny, setting long and short term goals, improving confidence, relaxing, and rehearsing mentally. It is a good book for coaches and players at every level."

"I think it should be required reading for all coaches."

TABLE OF CONTENTS

PREFACE

Much has happened since 1994 when we printed our second edition of <u>Power Play.</u> The New York Rangers won their first Stanley Cup since 1940 and the NHL has actually become 'trendy', high in both excitement and fashion.

The Colorado Avalanche and Detroit Red Wings have enjoyed success, the Pittsburgh Penguins experienced a strong regular season (1997 - 1998), and ex-Rochester player, Shjon Podein, has become a force in the NHL. Jim Johannson coached in the USHL. He took a team of USHL players to Germany and won the Junior Tournament. Mike Aikens is making his debut as a head coach in the USHL, coaching the Rochester Mustangs.

We sold out our first and second printing of <u>Power Play.</u> Rather than simply print more books, we've decided to keep updating our readers with a third edition. We've added some new anecdotes and a few new chapters and have inserted results from our research where appropriate. Athletic Guide Publishing will assume publishing and distribution responsibilities.

<u>Power Play</u> applies sport psychology to hockey, attempting in the process to correctly represent both the academic discipline of sport psychology and the game of hockey. The profits from <u>Power Play</u> were used for the first two <u>Power Play</u> scholarship awards in 1996-1997. The USHL recipients were Jeff Bernard of the Rochester Mustangs and T.J. Guidarelli of the Twin Cities Vulcan's.

As stated by Larry Wall and Kathleen Russell (1992),

"The road to success is always under construction."

Women's Hockey

The following two pictures are a tribute to women's hockey, which has been an organized sport longer than many think.

The first picture shows the Duluth girls hockey team in 1926 or 1927. Amy Dahl, who later married to become Amy Olsen, is the goalie. Amy will be 90 on January 20, 2000. When she was 80, she was giving ice skating lessons to pre-schoolers. She hung up her skates 3 years ago. Last spring she moved into a new house. She is active in church and works as a volunteer at a local hospital. She still travels and entertains frequently. Proud daughter, Priscilla (Pixy) Russell is employed at Mayo Clinic, Rochester, Minnesota in the Department of Communications.

Another example of women in sport over 75 years ago is this picture of my mother's ice hockey and basketball teams. Irene Isabel Stephens (nee White) is pictured in her skates on the far right. Prince Albert, Saskatchewan, Canada in 1923.

IT HAPPENED HERE　　　　　　　by Edith Petersen
Stanley Cup Games a gruelling experience in 1903

If modern hockey players had to work as hard as their predecessors did in the early days of Stanley Cup competition, they probably wouldn't have the energy or the inclination for the brawls and fisti cuffs they indulge in today. For there were no second strings then. There were seven men to a team and every man played the whole time unless seriously hurt. One of two substitutes were allowed in case of broken legs or really incapacitating injuries. There were two long periods with a break at half-time.

Naturally the players were pretty tired by the time a game was over and if there was overtime it was a gruelling experience.

Take, for instance, the Stanley Cup playoffs in 1903; the Winnipeg Victorias against the Montreal Hockey Club. The games were played at the Westmount Arena in Montreal, four of them in six days!

With no artificial ice, the season was shorter than now and the first game of the series took place Thursday, Jan. 29. But a sudden mild spell had ruined the ice, which was covered with about four inches of slush. Whenever a player took a shot, a spray of water covered everything in range. The Winnipeggers joked that they were not accustomed to playing in water and suggested they should have sent the Winnipeg Rowing Club's hockey team instead.

The Winnipeg players were: goal, Olson (first name not available); point, Roderick Flett; cover point, Magnus Flett; rover Billy Keen; centre, Fred Cadham (captain); right wing, A.B. (Tony) Gringras; left wing, Fred Scanlan.

As was learned later, Cadham was suffering from tonsillitis and Olson was also under the weather, but they played anyway. The game was held up early in the second half while three stitches were put in a cut over Rod Flett's eye. (Although. punches were not traded the way they are today, the games were wide open, rough and tough and sometimes downright dirty.)

Winnipeg was not accustomed to soft ice and lost to the heavier Montrealers, 8 to 1, a disastrous beginning for the Victorias.

The second game took place two days later, on Saturday night. Cold weather had firmed the ice and the Press sports writer W.G. Allan wired to the eager fans waiting for news at home: "The second game of the Stanley Cup struggle of 1903 will go down in history as one of the greatest exhibitions of hockey ever seen on Canadian ice. It was another instance of a Western cyclone sweeping down on the East and knocking all their calculations, their pointed sarcasms and incidentally, their 'men of iron' into a cocked hat.

Five minutes before time was up it looked as if the Vics must lose. The score 2-0 against them, although on the general play the Winnipeggers had proved themselves the superior team. But the plucky Westerners would not be denied and finally a brilliant rush by Scanlan and Gringras gave the latter an opening and he scored with a sizzling shot from right wing."

A few seconds later, Cadham scored on a pass from Gringras. According to Mr. Allan, "Cadham then started in to duplicate his scoring feat, but went down like an ox with a slash on the head. He staggered to his feet but declined to go to the dressing room, and resumed play like the great little bunch of nerve he is."

The gong rang and Winnipeg wanted to start the overtime immediately, but it was a few minutes before they got going again.

As Mr. Allan described it: "Montreal started to quibble and argue, playing for time. Finally they got on the ice again and play continued for half an hour, but it was of a heartrending description. It was killing hockey and although both teams struggled gamely, the pace could not be maintained and the players were falling all over the ice..."

The game was halted when a Montreal man went down with a crack over the knee that temporarily put him out of business. It was six minutes before midnight when the teams came back on the ice. (The game had started at 8:30 p.m.!) The players were so exhausted they could hardly skate.

But they were "saved by the gong" literally. There were strict Sabbath observance laws in Westmount and sharp at midnight the mayor pulled the rope that rang the gong to stop the game.

No one regretted that it was over and the tension was relieved. It was a tired but happy Winnipeg team that climbed into bed that night. Magnus Flett had to be put to bed and Keene and Scanlan were very sore. But Gringras, Rod Flett and Olson were in better shape, with only a few bruises and cuts.

Montreal tried to claim the cup on the grounds of having won one game and tied another. But the official decided the teams should play again on Monday.

At first it was announced that Saturday's overtime game should be finished first, to be followed immediately by another full game if Winnipeg won the overtime.

However, this meant that if Montreal won by scoring a sudden-death goal, perhaps in minutes or even a few seconds, there would be no need for another qame so the fans would feel cheated. So it was decided to play a full game, to be followed by a resumption of Saturday overtime game if necessary.

Although both teams showed the effects of Saturday's terrible struggle, the pace of Monday's game was fast and the play was sometimes quite brilliant. Keene scored three times and Scanlan once, to defeat Montreal, 4-1. So the teams were even.

The fourth game took place Wednesday. In Winnipeg about 1,000 men and boys were assembled as nearby as they could get to the Free Press building on McDermot Avenue, cramming the streets in every direction. Bulletins hot off the wires were thrown onto a large screen a new-fangled "stereoptical machine," and were all read through a megaphone.

The ice was soft again, giving Montreal the advantage over the lighter Winnipeg boys. A groan went up from the crowd at the Free Press when it was announced quite early in the game, that Cadham, with a cut over one eye and one foot bleeding badly from a skate cut, had fainted and had to leave the ice.

Dan Flett, the substitute, came out, but Winnipeg never got going again after that, and lost, 4-1. The cup stayed in Montreal.

One wonders how today's million-dollars boys would stand up to play like that.

(Found among the Smith-Cadham archivessource unknown.) The last comment does not necessarily reflect this author's opinion.

1

INTRODUCTION

Ice hockey is the fastest of all contact sports. Players skate at over 30 miles per hour, shoot pucks faster than a baseball pitcher can throw a fastball, and frequently collide with each other, the ice, and the boards. Hockey requires the individual player to possess skill, speed, strength, balance, and endurance. But hockey is also a team sport. It requires that individuals blend their talents to work toward common team goals. Real teamwork occurs when individual players simultaneously and successfully carry out their different assignments, whether their positions be center, wing, defense, or goalie. At the professional level, where there is great pressure to win games and fill seats, a team that can harness and develop individual talent and still focus on teamwork has the most success. Hockey teams need specialized players such as the high scorers and the tough, competitive 'grinders' who must win the physical battles for the puck along the boards and in the corners. Other players, sometimes known as policemen or enforcers, must provide intimidation and be prepared to fight in certain situations.[1] So although the game demands a high degree of grace, strength, and skill, hockey players learn that the game has strong components of physical and mental duress.

When we watch a game of hockey, all we see are the fluid movements of pucks, skates, and bodies, yet hockey players know that the physical aspects of the game go hand-in-hand with its mental aspects. Smart hockey players learn to read the game, to anticipate the movements of other players, and to understand the factors that influence their performances.

---

[1] Smith, Michael D. *Sources of Violence in Ice Hockey,* in <u>Children in Sport, 1988.</u>

Players who use their minds to enhance the performance of their bodies and who are under emotional control are "mentally tough" or "mentally fit". Unfortunately, many players fail to recognize the importance of the mental aspects of the game, which often keeps potentially good players from realizing their true ability. Consequently, this manual concentrates on hockey and how to master the mental aspects of the game.

HISTORY

Ice hockey originated and evolved into its highest level in Canada. For many years almost every player, manager, coach, and trainer in the National Hockey League was Canadian born.[2] In its early days, hockey was played with 6-man teams while indoor hockey rinks had not yet been invented. Yet as early as 1903, the sport had become a tough, fast, and grueling game. A newspaper account (included in earlier appendices) of the 1903 Stanley Cup is of particular interest to me, as Fred Cadham, captain of the Winnipeg Victorias, was my husband's grandfather.

Historically, the Canadians dominated the game of ice hockey until the years after WW II Following the war, the Soviets, who played a similar game called *Bandy,* became attracted to ice hockey. The Soviets and other European teams gradually developed great appreciation and expertise at the game which led to the appearance of hockey leagues, national teams, and international respect. The Canadians, however, virtually ignored the existence of hockey outside of Canada until 1972 when the Soviet amateur team came very close to defeating Team Canada. Other countries such as Czechoslovakia, Latvia, Sweden, Poland, Germany, Finland, Switzerland, and the United States continued to develop their amateur hockey programs. For example, Sweden, a country

---

[2] Fischler, Stan. *Golden Ice.* (MacGraw Hill: Scarborough, Ont. 1990) p.73.

not much bigger than the state of Minnesota, has more than 224 hockey arenas and over 750 hockey clubs. This embracing of hockey led to the development of increasingly skilled players and teams competing at the international level. The 1992 Winter Olympics showcased the skill and speed of the Unified hockey team (USSR) which defeated an excellent Canadian team to win the much coveted gold medal.

But twelve years earlier, in 1980, the United States shocked the world by defeating the Soviet Union and later Finland to win the Olympic Gold Medal in what is now known as the "Miracle on Ice." The winning team was comprised of American born players and it had an American born coach, Herb Brooks. Since 1980, a growing number of American youngsters are taking up the sport of hockey, and more than 18,000 teams are currently registered with USA Hockey. In Canada, it is estimated that 60,000 youngsters play minor league hockey in the province of Ontario and approximately 57,340 players participate in Quebec (Marcotte & Simard, 1993). Old-timer leagues flourish in both countries, made up of former youth, high school, college, and professional players, such as NHL goaltending great Ken Dryden, who play out of their continuing respect and enjoyment of the game.

Women's Ice Hockey is also expanding and there are now 58 teams at the College/University level. Furthermore, in '91 and '92, the International Ice Hockey Federation held Women's World Hockey Championships[3] and women's hockey was a medal sport in the 1998 Olympics. The USA Women won the gold medal after a hardfought battle with the Canadians. The caliber of play was excellent. Cammy Granato, Karyn Bye, and the rest of the USA women became heroes for the young girls and women who watched. Their victory was even sweeter because it was a disappointing year for both the American and Canadian men's teams, neither of whom were able to penetrate the Czechoslovakian goalie, Dominique

---

[3] Greer, Nancy, Dr. *Personal Communication*

Hasek, who regularly plays in the NHL with the Buffalo Sabres. The women's national hockey and soccer teams (winner of the World Cup) brought great honor and respect to women's sports. Readers are referred to <u>Proud Past, Bright Future: One Hundred Years of Canadian Women's Hockey</u> by Brian McFalone for a complete history of women's ice hockey. As an aside, Hasek was a "wall" during the Olympics in 1998. Not surprisingly, he and Ed Belfour of the Dallas Stars battled in the 1999 Stanley Cup finals. They forced the series to seven games and three overtimes before the Dallas Stars won on what many believe was a controversial goal.

Although coaches are adept at teaching physical hockey skills to players, the instruction and development of important mental skills rarely receives equal attention. Even at the NHL level where players and coaches receive huge salaries and media coverage and the expectations are high, too few franchises offer players assistance in handling performance anxiety. Players are often left on their own to learn how to deal with increasing performance pressures. As a result, players have difficulty executing skills well under the bright lights and cameras which serve only to increase the stress associated with constant performance evaluation. Friends and family, despite their love and support, are usually at a loss to help. They may contribute to a players' anxiety by expressing confidence in the player which the player might not feel. This tends to make the player feel alienated and somewhat of an impostor or a sham. Performance insecurities such as..."What if I blow it"... "I'm not really that good"...or "I've just been lucky", may dominate an athlete's thoughts.

SPORT PSYCHOLOGY TODAY

The following is just a short list of the professional and amateur athletes and teams which have begun to take action in addressing the mental aspects of performance in both individual and team sports. Managers and coaches have found that the mental aspects of athletics are best addressed by engaging the services of sport psychology consultants. The 1991 World Series brought into the spotlight educational sport psychologist Dr. Jack Lewallen, who discussed his efforts to help balance the mental states of Atlanta Braves pitcher, John Smoltz. The Boston Celtics employed Dr. Len Zaichowsky and many of the PGA golfers use the services of Dr. Bob Rotella.

The Olympic training center employs two sport psychologists, who assist elite athletes with the pressures of high level competition. According to the news media, Payne Stewart, winner of the 1991 U.S. Open, was traveling to major tournaments with a sport psychologist, and Dr. Debra Crews, a golf expert, works with the LPGA. Nancy Kerrigan sought assistance from sport psychologist, Cindy Adams, (Kerrigan, 1994) who undoubtedly helped her stay focused after the "Tanya Tap"! NHL teams such as the Montreal Canadiens, the Boston Bruins, the New York Islanders, the Vancouver Canucks, the Detroit Red Wings, and the Chicago Blackhawks have reportedly used team sport psychology consultants such as Dr. Wayne Halliwell and Dr. Cal Botterill to enhance performance and increase team cohesion.

Sport Psychologist Dr. Cal Botterill was interviewed in a Winnipeg paper and commented on the need to help the New York Rangers regain confidence after having too easily been defeated in their 1993 play-off series. They succeeded in winning a Stanley Cup a few years later. Apparently, ESPN analyst and hockey expert Barry Melrose, who once coached the LA Kings, was a believer in motivational guru Tony Robbins and enlisted his support to help keep the Kings pumped and focused during their drive to and during the Stanley Cup playoffs a few years ago. Introducing techniques to athletes to help them control their thoughts and emotions under pressure along with helping them develop their pure physical ability, is the wave of the future in sports.

Power Play is about thinking (cognition) and feeling (emotion) and about how those two factors affect hockey performance. It will teach positive strategies for gaining control, accepting one's role, goal setting, relaxation, imagery, confidence, concentration, and the enhancement of team cohesion. Power Play also explains the principles of arousal level, optimal flow zone, leadership, peak performance, coach and player relationships, maintaining success, and provides some insights on the prevention and rehabilitation of sports injuries. Practical examples, exercises, and initiatives are provided to enhance and reinforce the hockey player's understanding of these concepts. In addition to experiential learning, self-tests appear at the beginning and end of certain chapters where mental skills are introduced. The topics of flexibility, hockey nutrition, and sports medicine for hockey will also be discussed. A section on goaltending includes references and comments on what we have discovered from our six years of research about this important position. Application of the concepts in Power Play should enable you to get into the game with your head, as well as with your body, regardless of your association to hockey.

2

HOCKEY-PLAYING OUT OF CONTROL

The control center of your life is your attitude.

Some of the true pressures in ice hockey are experienced by young NHL draft picks, rookies trying to "stick with the team," veterans trying to hold on for another year or two, teams during play-offs and important games, as well as coaches and general managers. According to author Dick Irvin, players and coaches on the Montreal Canadiens are expected to live up to the tradition of those who went before them. Pictures of previous Stanley Cup teams hanging in the Forum reminded coaches that Dick Irvin, Toe Blake, and Scotty Bowman did a fair amount of winning in their day. When Pat Burns was coaching the Montreal Canadiens (1988-1992) he said, "The first time I walked into the dressing room as the coach, I was shaking, I mean really shaking."[4] When serving as general manager of the New York Rangers, Phil Esposito said that his new role had made him "a totally obsessive workaholic. You have to be mentally tough no matter where you are or what you do, you've got to be strong mentally to succeed."[5] Borje Salming, in his autobiography, writes that "as my NHL debut neared, I was nervous."[6] Other players write about throwing up in the bathrooms before the game. Goaltender Gump Worsely developed ulcers. Despite this obvious difficulty in dealing with performance pressures, when Salming wrote about his 17 years in the NHL he stated

---

[4] Irvin, D. *The HABS.* (McClelland & Stewart, Inc.: Toronto, Canada. 1992)

[5] Howe, C., Howe, G. and Wilkins, C. *After the Applause.* (McClelland & Stewart, Inc.: Toronto, Canada. 1990) p. 87

[6] Salming, B. and Karlsson, G. *Blood, Sweat and Hockey.* (Haper Collins Publishers, Ltd.: Toronto, Canada. 1991)

that "the key to play-off success in the NHL lies less in skating and playmaking than in learning to cope with extreme pressure. Players must be able to stay calm, concentrate on the task at hand, and not get caught up in the hysteria."[7]

Even Wayne Gretzky admitted to feeling pressure and was rarely able to score on a penalty shot. Why did this happen when Gretzky could usually finesse his way past both defensemen and goaltenders? If he could score more frequently than any other player under normal conditions, why did a one-on-one with a goaltender cause such a problem'? Was it that Gretzky never developed the physical skills for these situations? Of course not. According to him, it was the mental response to the pressure of being alone on the ice one-on-one with too much time to think and to 'psych himself out'.

PLAYERS OF TODAY

Today's hockey players may be better than those of yesteryear, but most have paid a high price. They have been influenced by parents, coaches, teammates, and friends and, consequently, they carry around a lot of unnecessary emotional 'baggage'. They are the products of hockey schools, zealous coaches, indoor arenas, and overly-involved parents. Today's players rarely step on the ice without having had lengthy chalk-talks and they are very aware that their performance will be thoroughly analyzed. In the NHL, each shift is criticized and mistakes are usually pointed out to players in front of their teammates. As a result, today's players are often long on strategy but short on skills confidence. The gains players have made in physical skills are frequently offset by their *fear of failure*. A fear of failure can sometimes lead to an athlete's being almost paralyzed by the anxiety of making mistakes and disappointing team members, family, coaches, and themselves.

[7] Salming, B. and Karlsson, G. Ibid.

Another contemporary problem for players' confidence is the length of the bench and the great depth of some teams. In the NHL, a minor league team has a full roster of players who are just dying to get the call! A poor performance, just a few mistakes and players often find themselves sitting out for weeks before they can work their way back into the lineup. Compare today's roster to the account from the 1903 Stanley Cup when each team had seven players and everyone played the whole time unless seriously hurt. "One or two substitutes were allowed in case of broken legs." (Appendix 1).

Because previous performance efficacy is an important predictor of subsequent performance, it is easy to understand why players say, "I haven't played enough to really get myself into the game." Consider Mike Richter, goalie for the New York Rangers, during their Stanley Cup winning play-offs, "While he appeared in the 1991-92 NHL All-Star Game, Richter's game lacked the polish and confidence that comes with playing every night. He bottomed out the following season and was sent back to Binghamton, the minor league team. His rebound during the 1993-94 season was a driving force in the Rangers' success and he was rewarded with lots of playing time."[8]

Prior to the 1990-91 World Junior tournament, one talented player, now playing regularly in the NHL, said that his greatest fear was making a mistake. Many of his teammates agreed with him. Recognizing that this was a common problem, we discussed in a team psychology meeting the consequences of a mistake he might make in hockey. By taking a confrontive "rational-emotive" approach and after some thought, the team concluded that the consequences of making a mistake are not as grave as they originally may seem. Unlike a surgeon, a pilot, or an obstetrician, people don't die as a result of a hockey player's mistakes and players can live

---

[8] Hockey Night in Toronto, Toronto Maple Leafs Official Game Magazine, 1994, p. 102

with the consequences of their errors. It is the fear itself, more than any of the possible consequences, which has the most power to intimidate the player.

But hockey is a game of great speed and split second timing and, therefore, it is a game of mistakes. The team who makes the least mistakes usually wins, but in order to win, the risk of making a mistake must be taken. All professional athletes make mistakes. Cal Ripkin struck out more than 797 times and yet, he is one of the best baseball players.[9]

The burden of hours of chalk talks and emphasis on theory may put a player facing a big game in a situation similar to that experienced before an important examination. 'A test! Do I know it or not'?' Unfortunately, many of the skills the player must possess to be an effective player are difficult and complex. These skills include controlled stick handling, intricate passing, skating speed, maneuverability, and endurance. Such skills are better executed when an athlete is in control and in a pumped up, yet relaxed state of both mind and body. The player who is uptight and worried is unable to get into the flow of the game. The consequences of pressure and anxiety may be responsible for a player's poor passing ability, early muscle fatigue, weak concentration, and a lack of anticipation. In other words, the player will not be able to *get into the game* both physically and mentally without the right mind-set.

Just the pressure of competing in the NHL World Championships, NCAA Tournaments, USHL Playoffs, or other important games or tryouts may be enough to throw a player off his game. Skills that are easy in practice may seem impossible to execute in a game. Last year one player told me that when he got called up from the minors to the NHL, he was so uptight, he couldn't settle down. He tried to do far too much and didn't simply "play his game" as he planned. Another player felt he was really just a kid in a grown man's

---

[9] Special Report, Kids in Sport, Jim Thorton, 1993

body. Most of last season I watched one promising USHL forward come up short on goals, releasing too soon or too late, the puck going everywhere but in the net. I watched the same player this season during tryouts for a team he was virtually assured of making, and he couldn't miss! He was relaxed, his stride was fluid and fast, and his hands were soft, his release quick. A different player'? No, the same player, but a different mind-set.

Although quick to identify psychological causes for poor performance, most coaches rarely feel comfortable enough with their knowledge of sport psychology to introduce emotional-control strategies to their players. This is understandable since it takes as long to learn about this discipline of sports science as it does to learn the art and science of coaching. Coaches who have played in the NHL probably best understand the emotions players experience. The New Jersey Devils were coached by Jacques Lemaire (voted 1994 NHL Coach of the Year) and Larry Robinson, a former defenseman for the Montreal Canadiens. It was not surprising to me to read that during the tough New Jersey-New York Ranger series, Stevens was quoted as saying, "Lemaire wants us to go out there, play our game, and have fun." I also understand that Lemaire generously directed much of the praise he received to his assistant coach, (who at the time was Larry Robinson, an ex-teammate), the sign of a person with a secure self-image.

Lindy Ruff, who had an excellent year coaching the Buffalo Sabres, played in the NHL for years. Except for a controversial goal in the Stanley Cup 7th game in the third overtime period, the Sabres might have claimed the 1999 Stanley Cup. However, Lindy's opponents were the Dallas North Stars, a team strongly influenced by their G.M., Bob Gainey, who was an outstanding defensive player with the Montreal Canadians. According to the media, when Mike Modano struggled with pressure he was putting on himself, he turned to Bob Gainey (one who had "been there") who helped put things into perspective.

For most players, mental toughness skills are not inherited and they cannot be learned by osmosis. They are *learned skills.*[10] Players can learn not to choke, pass blindly, or miss the body check at key times *if they choose to learn.* It is said that the most important part of a player is located above the shoulders, meaning his or her head. Yet even though we understand how important the mental aspects of the game are, not all of today's hockey players have had access to sport psychology or to a quality mental toughness program to help them handle pressure, have fun, play in control, and play at their best.

As one former NHL player told me, "we were supposed to automatically know how to handle the pressure, and we didn't." Fear of failing, of not living up to expectations and of letting down other players, the fans, or the coach promotes the same 'defensive shell' in an individual that is too often seen in teams that find themselves in the lead during the final period of a close game. When highly concerned about making an error and giving up a goal, players freeze, slow down, fail to execute, and may end up losing a game that they deserved and planned to win. This mental mode obviously removes both the individual and the team from an offensive position and predisposes both to problems.

The following chapters in <u>Power Play</u> address strategies that will help you acquire and maintain a sense of control throughout your career and will lead to on and off-ice hockey experiences that are challenging, fun, and rewarding.

"Success comes to those who make it happen not to those who let it happen."

---

[10] Loehr, J. Mental Toughness. (Penguin Books: New York, NY. 1982)

3

REGAINING CONTROL AND ACCEPTING RESPONSIBILITY

There is a time when we must firmly choose the course we will follow or the endless drift of events will make the decision for us –Prochnow

As stated earlier, mental toughness is a learned skill. Hockey players didn't learn to skate without first being ankle runners and falling many times. It takes years of practice to perfect difficult hockey skills. Similarly, mental toughness skills are learned by working at them and practicing. By directing oneself toward mental control and positive thoughts, a hockey player can gradually achieve the poise and on-ice control desired. While you cannot change what was given to you by nature — such as your height, facial features, or innate athletic ability — you can learn to change your present level of mental toughness. In other words, you can learn to control how intensely, aggressively, tenaciously, and courageously you play the game. To do this, you must identify which mental toughness skills need to be improved.

It is said that improvement begins with the letter 'I'

SELF-TEST # 1.1
(Do your best to answer the questions even though you may not be familiar with these concepts. See if your ability to answer the questions has increased by the time you complete the Self-Test at the end of the chapter)

1. Rate your knowledge of Attribution Theory or the need to take control.

1	2	3	4	5
very low				*very high*

2. Rate your belief about the importance of Attribution Theory or the need to take control.

1	2	3	4	5
very low				*very high*

3. Rate your planned use of Attribution Theory or the need to take control.

1	2	3	4	5
very low				*very high*

UNDERSTANDING OUR OWN BEHAVIOR

In a nutshell, you must learn to understand yourself. If you can identify specific changes you wish to make, you can be taught certain strategies to enhance or modify that behavior[11]. To understand the benefits of these strategies introduced to modify certain behaviors, you can begin to monitor your performance and thereby evaluate the effectiveness of the changes made. For example, some players have difficulty controlling their tempers. Lack of anger control can impair on-ice performance or keep professional coaches from playing certain players in high pressure situations. By discussing aspects of the player's behavior, such as when anger occurs, why it happens, and how it was reinforced, the undesirable behavior will become clearer to the player. A program can be designed to modify the undesirable behavior. The goal is emotional control, and the player must develop the capacity to walk away from fights or situations counterproductive to the team's goals. Unfortunately, the demands of the game at some levels of participation require that other players increase their toughness and feistiness. Regardless of which

---

[11] Gould, D., Petlichkoff, L., Hodge, K. and Simons, J.. Evaluating the Effectiveness of a Psychological Skills Educational Workshop. (The Sport Psychologist 4, 1990) p. 249-260.

way on the continuum you are trying to go, your behaviors must be controlled. A talented player who has himself under good emotional control will be more effective and beneficial to the team than a player who is out of emotional control. Furthermore, the player who has control is likely to go farther in a hockey career because his play will be more consistent.

A useful psychology theory, called Attribution Theory, can be applied to accepting responsibility for one's behavior in hockey and in life.

Figure 1.

	INTERNAL	EXTERNAL	
STABLE	ABILITY	TASK	
UNSTABLE	EFFORT	LUCK	

ATTRIBUTION THEORY

Hockey players can credit or blame either the internal (ability and effort) or external (task and luck) components of this model for their successes or failures. One research study of downhill ski racers helps us to understand the message of these little boxes.

WINNERS

Research has shown that successful ski racers (winners) tend to attribute both success and failure to the internal components of *ability* and *effort.* When they won, the skiers believed it was due to their hard work in developing their *ability* and that they had made a concentrated, committed *effort.* When they lost, which was not often, it was because they believed they had not skied up to their ability or that they had failed to give a full effort.

LOSERS

In the same study, those who lost more than they won attributed their rare successes to external factors such as luck or that the race course (task) was easy. When they lost, which occurred fairly regularly, it was because the course (task) was too hard or because visibility was bad (luck). They failed to recognize that the skiers who won competed under the same conditions.

INTERPRETATION OF THE ATTRIBUTION THEORY

The 'winners' who focused on internal characteristics kept their emphasis on what was under their power to control or to change. Ability and effort can always be modified by realizing the problem and then providing oneself with the means to correct it. For example, one skier might have thought 'I should have kept my weight on the downhill ski. I will practice that run 10 times tomorrow to make that correction.'

APPLICATION TO HOCKEY

This model applies well to hockey. You, as a hockey player, also play your best by keeping your focus on *ability* and *effort.* This is due to the simple fact that *ability* and *effort* are the most important factors which you have the power to change or control. Success is then measured against your internal yardstick and is independent of such things as a referee's call, slow ice, or a lucky deflection. While those factors can and do influence the outcome of a game, long-run successes almost always occur when you meet the goals you set for yourself that are within your power to achieve. You have the power to create and meet such goals as putting hard, low shots on net, making solid checks, winning face offs, and performing with a consistent work ethic in the less glamorous skills of back-checking and digging out the puck from in the corners. Taking responsibility for your performance enables you to objectively and constructively evaluate your performance and set corrective goals for the next practice. Taking that responsibility is the sign of a winner's attitude. Even very good hockey players sometimes find it hard to accept responsibility for their failures. When the Toronto Maple Leafs let the Philadelphia Flyers steal their 5-2 lead in the last six minutes of an important game, Salming screamed at his coach, Red Kelly, "Why did you say, we've got them'? It's your job to keep us playing hard until the game is over!" Later Salming apologized for his outburst and accepted responsibility, acknowledging that the coach hadn't lost the game; it was the players.

On the other hand, during the final round of the 1993-94 Stanley Cup Playoffs, Mark Messier took a huge risk in predicting a win for the Rangers. His comments did not escape the media! Although he acknowledged his intent was not to be prophetic, but to unify and instill confidence in his team, he 'cooly' contributed a hat trick to the team effort. Thus, he assumed responsibility, neither making excuses nor deflecting responsibility to the coach, media, fans, or blaming playing conditions. A few years ago, Patrick Roy left the Montreal Canadiens to join the Colorado Avalanche. It was expected that he would contribute to his team's successes. One of the coaches or players from an opposing team deliberately tried to take him "off his game" by making critical and embarrassing statements. When asked what he thought of the disparaging remarks, he said he wasn't able to hear too well because he had his "Stanley Cup rings in his ears!" Roy refused to give up control or "fall for the ploy." Instead, he kept his focus until the end of the Stanley Cup Playoffs when the team rewarded the Colorado Avalanche fans with the Stanley Cup.

Players who attribute their performance to the external components of *task* and *luck* have a tendency to absolve themselves of responsibility by claiming that 'the other team was too tough' or 'we failed to get the breaks, bad luck.' By giving away responsibility, these players are not providing themselves with a blueprint for improvement. They will simply wait to get lucky or wait to play an easier team. Players go nowhere when they make excuses and refuse to be accountable for their successes and failures. As a hockey player, you should ask yourself whether you accept responsibility or deflect it.

A LESSON LEARNED

After the Edmonton Oilers suffered a disappointing loss in the Stanley Cup finals a few years ago, Wayne Gretzky and Kevin Lowe happened to walk by the winner's locker room, Gretzky described in his book what he saw and how he felt. They looked into their opponents' dressing room expecting to see a party in action, with champagne and great celebration. Instead, they looked in and saw Denis Potvin applying an ice bag to a huge cut while another player was getting stitched up by the team physician. Still another player was being examined by the trainer. Kevin Lowe turned to Gretzky and said, "You see, that's why they won and we didn't. They gave it all they had."[12] It is interesting to note that for the next several years Edmonton won the Stanley Cup. They had learned the harsh lesson of what is takes to be a championship

---

[12] Gretzky, Wayne. An Autobiography. (Harper-Collins Publishers: New York, NY 1990) p. 154.

team in the NHL's Stanley Cup playoffs.

GRETZKY, AS AN EXAMPLE

Wayne Gretzky was a good example of an *internal* attributer (someone who took full responsibility for his own ability and effort) in hockey. Year after year, he set his own performance expectations in terms of specific goal points and assist points. He planned to meet his personal performance goals and usually did. When skating with Gretzky on Team Canada, Mario Lemieux commented that he was astounded at the effort Gretzky expended during every practice and every game. Apparently, Gretzky took pride in his many successes and full responsibility for his occasional failures.

Gretzky was sold to the Edmonton Oilers from the Indianapolis Racers when he was 17 years of age. In Edmonton, he chalked up 46 goals and 64 assists in his rookie year. Even so, Glen Sather, the Oiler coach, (in 1998 Sather was the most sought after General Manager in the NHL before resigning with the Edmonton Oilers, a team with new ownership who have pledged some resources to success) had to be vigilant in dealing with Gretzky's defensive flaws which he considered to be the only weak part of the rookie's game. During one game, 'the rookie' made a defensive blunder and returned to the bench to wait for his next turn on the ice. The turn never came. He sat on the bench for the remainder of that period and the next period until Sather felt the lesson had been learned. According to Sather, "He could have pouted and sulked, but no way." Gretzky scored a hat trick in the third period, enabling the Oilers to win 5-2.[13] He obviously accepted the responsibility for his error and realized he was benched because of his lack of defensive effort. He accepted the challenge, kept his focus on controlling his ability and effort, and avoided the trap of the loser which is to blame bad luck, the coach, or the referee. All players must strive for

[13] Fischler, Stan, ibid.

the maturity and the self-understanding needed to accept full responsibility for each and every performance. Being able to do that also signifies that a player is truly coachable.

A young player I know lost a year of eligibility in college and experienced major disappointments during his early Junior career. Instead of "giving up or in", he tightened his resolve, earned a scholarship, was selected captain of a Division I hockey team, and was named the conference's best defensive forward. He then experienced a very successful minor league season. This player has the mental attitude of a winner and kept the quotation, "Anything less than my best is unworthy of me" on his desk while attending university.

NBA basketball fans will recall the thrilling see-saw 1998 NBA finals. Both Karl Malone and Michael Jordon had publicly accepted responsibility for ensuring their teams would be successful. Both players had some great moments until the Chicago Bulls really pulled together (Rodman included) to put the final game "away"!

Excuses are the tools with which persons with no purpose in view build for themselves great monuments of nothing

REASONS FOR NOT ACCEPTING RESPONSIBILITY

1. To protect one's image and reputation as a skilled hockey player.

2. To avoid being criticized. This is often felt by players who have a strong need for approval of others.

3. To maintain feelings of superiority. Players may tell themselves, 'I couldn't make a mistake like that.'

4. To lessen the hurt one experiences after a mistake or a poor performance that lets down oneself and the team.

COMMON EXCUSES OR RATIONALIZATIONS

1. Ice conditions are terrible.

2. The referee is biased.

3. The linesman didn't call the offside.

4. I was tripped and it wasn't called.

5. The coach has been skating us too hard and I was too tired.

6. 'I can't come in cold just when he (the coach) wants me to' and 'I don't have my head in the game'.

7. My linemates can't keep up to me, and they lose the puck.

8. I don't play well when we are traveling.

9. I don't get enough ice time to play well.

10. We never win or play well in this arena or on the road.

Don't make excuses, make good!

Mentally tough teams turn adversity into a challenge and accept full responsibility for their performance. The 1991 NCAA Hockey Championship was won by the University of Northern Michigan. At the last moment, they were unable to fly to Minneapolis, the site of the championship playoffs, because their plane was unable to take off in fog. Consequently, the players were loaded onto buses for the long trip from Marquette, Michigan to Minneapolis. The players unloaded with stiff, cramped legs but when they went on the ice, they defeated Clarkson and Boston College (in 3 overtimes) to win the NCAA championship! They didn't make excuses, the Northern Michigan team made good.

Similarly, I believe Lake Superior State won the NCAA Championship three times in the past several years. Apparently, instead of seeing themselves as a "little school of 2000 students," they turned this fact into a mental advantage. By pulling together perfectly, they saw themselves as a David, their opponents as Goliath (big, but vulnerable!).

Brad Marsh, whose career spanned 1,086 games, toiling on the blue line for six different teams expressed it this way, "I understood my game and what I could and couldn't do. I didn't let what I couldn't do affect what I could do. In my mind I knew that I was strong in front of my net, in the corner, getting the puck out of my zone. Each night I tried to do those simple things to the best of my ability." Don Cherry said of this player, "Show me a player who has heart and soul and puts the team number one, and I'll show you a Brad Marsh." (Sports Canada, 1993). Other players such as Joe Sakic (Colorado Avalanche) and Steve Yzerman (Detroit Red Wings) have earned similar reputations.

Perhaps this past season Dallas Star Mike Modano "shone" the brightest as the ultimate team player. He continued to contribute to his team both offensively and defensively throughout the Stanley Cup playoff final in spite of a damaged and painful wrist.

ACCEPT RESPONSIBILITY FOR YOUR PERFORMANCE FACTORS YOU CAN CONTROL:

1. Have a realistic plan of what you wish to do in each practice or game.

2. Practice assertively and excitedly with an emotional level similar to what you would want in a game. (Get your body used to performing under a consistent level of arousal).

3. Mentally prepare in advance for the opposing team and know:
   - their goaltender's strengths and weaknesses
   - characteristics of the forwards and defense you will play against
   - prepare for factors such as the presence of general managers, media hype, scouts, or the cheering/booing of fans

4. Mentally prepare for your line's play (anticipating the style, habits, and preferences of linemates) know whom to lead on a pass, know who plays the boards, know how your center takes the face off.

5. Be prepared for all types of coaching situations. Injuries or illnesses may occur, someone on your line may not play well, or your line may be benched. Don't get down. Plan to stay up and ready to go. Ask yourself how Podein, Deadmarsh, Adam Oates, Lindros, Hasek, Modano, Bye, or Granato would have handled it'?

6. Avoid criticizing your linemates when they make errors. Every hockey player makes errors and it might be you next time. We all chastise ourselves enough-what we all need is encouragement. Be positive.

7. Avoid being intimidated by another team's reputation, their size or the color of their uniforms. Remember, David took down Goliath, and the Sharks not only took the first playoff round from Detroit (1993-94), they also took Toronto to seven games. The year before they had

the worst record of any team <u>ever</u> in the NHL.

8. Plan to concentrate by keeping your focus, your eye on the puck and avoid being taken out of your game by being drawn offside mentally, into penalties, or fights. *You can't meet your goals if you are in the penalty box.* Remember the anecdote about Patrick Roy and his Stanley Cup rings. Recognize and resist your opponents' attempts to get you rattled.

9. Plan to avoid equipment problems. Keep your sticks within the legal curvature. Keep your skates sharpened and make sure all of your padding is comfortable and not a distraction to you.

FACTORS OUT OF YOUR CONTROL

1. You cannot control the line your coach plays you on (you can work to play on a particular line, but the coach may, for example, need your defensive skills or offensive skills on a different line).

2. You cannot control when your line gets benched because a linemate is having an off game, although good communication may help prevent this. If it is your error that caused the benching, focus immediately on how to prevent that error the next time. Figure out whether or not your *ability* and *effort will* prevent a similar mistake. Learn from mistakes made by both you and your linemates. Watch the game closely!

3. You probably cannot control bad calls from referees. Simply take them in stride. Let your coach deal with bad calls. Your task is to focus immediately on the next shift, on the positive, on what you can control.

In conclusion, accepting responsibility for your performance in hockey and in life is the cornerstone or foundation upon which this book is based. Once that principle is grasped, the remainder of this book is easy and simply provides strategies to improve on areas that need work or to further enhance your strengths as a player. You can then prepare for each hockey game confident in your ability to be accountable for your performance.

If it is to be, it is up to me!

Exercise 1

Situations and Attributions

Using the Attribution Boxes

Internal	External	
Ability	Task	Stable
Effort	Luck	Unstable

For the following hypothetical situation in a hockey game, pick from the numbered statements that follow and match the correct number with the correct box or boxes. A statement may have more than one answer.

Example: You take a cross checking penalty and go to the penalty box during the last 10 minutes of an important game when the score is tied at 2:2.

ATTRIBUTIONS

1. I was really unlucky to get caught. The referee just happened to turn and see me then.
2. If I had practiced my power starts a bit more, I could have accelerated faster, and would have been ahead instead of behind him on that play. I need to set some goals to keep my stick down to ensure I don't cross check.
3. I have to make a real attempt at staying emotionally even. My opponent has been hooking me all night and I let him get to me. I need to "channel click" (Chapter 7).
4. Talk about the breaks, this always happens to me. Now, I'll probably get benched and it really wasn't my fault.
5. I am a better skater than that. I could have beaten him to the puck. I have to focus on getting a "jump start." I'll set a goal to work on faster starts.
6. The other player was just too good and I couldn't stop him any other way. Besides, he deserved it.

ANSWERS:

Ability	2, 5
Effort	2, 3, 5
Task	6
Luck	1, 4

SELF-TEST # 1.2

1. Rate your knowledge of Attribution Theory or the need to take control.

1	2	3	4	5
very low				very high

2. Rate your belief about the importance of Attribution Theory or the need to take control.

1	2	3	4	5
very low				very high

3. Rate your planned use of Attribution Theory or the need to take control.

1	2	3	4	5
very low				very high

4

COACHABILITY

"Accept your limitations and they shall be yours."
Richard Bach

QUESTION: **What does being coachable really mean?**

ANSWER: **Letting go, developing trust, and making a fast transition!**

INTRODUCTION

Being coachable means "letting go of old beliefs" that you have held all your life. Those beliefs are reinforced constantly by families, friends, and your past success. As a hockey player and athlete, you have developed a sense of who you are based on what you feel, what you see, and what people said you could be. Unfortunately, that's the player you *were.* It's the past, but it's not the *now,* it's not the *future,* and it probably isn't what's best for you.

What am I talking about? Your skills and resources and the demands of the game change at every level and during every week, month, and season. You have to make the mental changes that are necessary. It's the same way with our personalities. How many of you used to be shy'? Maybe you were shy but now your teammates may say you never stop talking, or maybe the opposite, you used to be outgoing and now you feel shy. As you grow and mature you will change, and you need to adjust accordingly to those changes. In Bantam maybe you were the best checker in the league and now you are board shy! How can that be?

THE ROLE THAT PLAYERS USED TO PLAY

You may have been a very fast skater as a kid, savvy, quick, and cute with the puck. Or perhaps you were big and slow, and your shot was a "nothing". Whatever you were, you formed a view of yourself as a hockey player. It's the image you have in your mind's eye of how you see yourself on the ice. Maybe you used to be your team's offensive defenseman and the anchor on the point in the power play. Perhaps that player is who you still think you are now, but that may no longer true. Things may have changed. In a new league at a different level it will matter whether or not you have grown or not grown, gotten faster or slower, weaker or stronger, and more or less courageous and confident relative to the other players in your league. You can't help or change all of that, but you must be open to a reassessment of who you are now. That means taking a hard look at the coach's view of you. That's scary, and often our tendency is to cling to what we 'were' when we felt good about ourselves, when we felt successful, when we were noticed and appreciated. But what was may no longer be true. Maybe as a player your mind hasn't 'let go'. Maybe deep down you don't believe you can change. Players sometimes set up so many mental barriers to change that they fail. They are afraid to change because new behaviors on ice and a new role feels awkward and clumsy. Players feel foolish, vulnerable, and hate making mistakes, so they unfortunately may not make as fast and as complete a physical and mental transition to change as the coach wants. Then, as a result of their on-ice behavior, they don't progress, don't grow, and don't get the ice time they want. Parents and significant others may not understand the awkwardness that they see during the steep learning curve. They may suggest that the players regress to what worked a year ago. Players can feel trapped, confused, indecisive, and lose their confidence. No! Don't! Embrace change! It is best to let go of what was and make as fast a transition as possible to what is expected now! Physically, your body will respond if you give it a clear message, are patient, determined, and enthusiastic.

A few years ago an NHL player who was well respected as a tough forward and a grinder felt vulnerable in his hockey career because he was classified as an "enforcer." In his opinion, he felt he could easily be replaced by any big goon willing to fight who might walk onto his team. We talked about how he had 'lit the light' in Canadian Major Junior before playing in the NHL. He was convinced he could never do that again, that he could not change roles so dramatically, and that he'd lost the skills necessary to score.

I told him that if I could become an accomplished wind surfer and take up 'telemark back country skiing' in middle age, he could not convince me that at 25 years of age he could not relearn how to score. I told him that the psychomotor skills that he'd known and learned well for 15 years could still be retrieved from motor memory if he wanted it badly enough! After making a real effort and taking a positive perspective, one year later he scored a hat trick in a Stanley Cup playoff game.

I don't know if his coach was happy with his becoming more offensive-minded than defensive-minded so his story is not meant as an example of "coachability", but rather as an example of how we can change and adapt. He was made captain of his team and enjoyed his NHL career as a less vulnerable, excellent two-way player.

A young forward who played in the USHL was identified by his coach as having promise as a defensive forward. He was "coachable", took the advice given him, and despite a difficult start that limited him as far as years of eligibility for a Division I scholarship, he received an offer. He was named "defensive player of the year" in the CCHA.

Some high school coaches told me a few years ago about a player who exemplified coachability. They described the following situation. After a bad game the coaches skated their players hard on outdoor ice to punish them for a bad game. After unloading the bus with the equipment bags, one player left (he'd been excused) carrying with him the wrong bag! The bag he left had skates about 4 or 5 sizes bigger than the skates in the bag he had taken. The player whose bag was taken did not say a word. He skated for two or three hours on slushy outdoor ice, taking his punishment without complaint. Not until the punishment skate was over did the coaches notice that the fastest player on the ice was wearing skates so big and sloppy that his ankles rolled over. Yet, he didn't whine, instead he made good.

THE ROLE THE PLAYER MUST PLAY NOW

The coach is the only person affiliated with the team who really knows objectively and in detail the strengths and weaknesses of each player and how your team will match up player-for-player with the opposition. Good coaches know who can cycle, pivot, pass, shoot, and check from the right and left sides and down low. Coaches have scouted, watched game tapes, watched tryouts, and have watched all players in practices. They can tell what aspects of your game must be improved before you can work your way into the lineup, onto a power play, or man short unit. Hockey is coached like an action packed chess game and players have to know and assume their roles.

When I worked with a professional NHL team and a minor league team, the coach lacked two defensive-minded defensemen. That year he coached all players to play 'the trap' with the exception of one line. The East European line was given permission to play offensively for their shift providing they kept a positive plus/minus. They were solid, skilled offensive players (some of the best in the world) but arguably they were not strong defensive players. The coach felt that if they could score some points, maintain puck control, which was a great strength of theirs, and run down the clock while allowing the lines who played the trap to rest and regroup, he could win some games. As the coach, he had not chosen most of the players (in the NHL, the General Manager has a lot of control), so it was an example of Robert Louis Stevenson's quotation:

Ask not that you be dealt a perfect hand, but rather that you play the poor hand well!

The players I am discussing were not poor players. Au contraire. It's simply that the coach's read of the NHL expansion team was that a tight defense was needed to stifle opponents. The coach was right and the NHL team came together and beat the Detroit Red Wings in the first round of the Stanley Cup. They then took Toronto to seven games in the second round. It was the most turned around season ever for a team in the NHL and their coach was nominated for coach of the year. A challenging task was trying to help players "accept" their roles, be coachable, let go of the old, and embrace change. Many North American players also "hate" the trap and resent it when they perceived the offensive opportunities were afforded only to the European players. At the NHL level, many contracts have bonuses for the number of goal and assist points, so the `trap' was initially resented because it seemed to offer fewer scoring opportunities. Gradually the players accepted their roles and played for the good of the team. But they could have had an even better season and drawn a higher play-off seed if they'd been a little more coachable and made a faster transition to their new roles.

So, trust the coaches! Recognize that they have watched you play, studied you either in person last season, on game tapes, or in training camps. The coaches selected you because they thought you could play and help this team – if you play a certain way, a certain role. So listen, learn, and embrace change!

THE SPEED OF THE TRANSITION IS WHAT COUNTS

Hopefully, while players on other teams are struggling with this issue, players on your team will seize the opportunity to benefit from coaching instruction. The following table contains strategies to help ease the transition.

TABLE 1

Steps to Being Coachable

1. Try to get a clear vision or image in your mind's eye of how the coaches want you to play.

2. After each practice make sure you understand exactly what was taught so that you know what to focus on.

3. If you are unsure, seek clarification from your coaches. Discuss what was emphasized in practice with your linemates so that you know how to incorporate what was taught. Physically condition to facilitate your adjustment to the role. For example, if more speed is needed, practice jump starts, power skating, sprints, anticipation, etc.

5. Use relaxation before imaging to help clear your mind and increase your focus and concentration.

6. Then practice mental imagery (seeing yourself in your mind's eye) to rehearse all drills such as checking, breakout passes, 3 on 2's, breakaways, saves, etc.
7. Ignore suggestions from anyone except the coaches.

8. Explain to your invested parents, siblings, or friends who give you conflicting advice that you appreciate their interest, but that at this level you can only benefit from the advice of the coaching staff on your team (coaches, teammates, trainers, counselors, etc.).

Carpe Diem!

5

GOAL SETTING

**Great Visions Start With Small Dream Goals...
Happiness Involves Working Towards Meaningful Goals**

No strategy offered in Sport Psychology is as simple and powerful as Goal Setting. Goal setting is a strong motivational technique. To be successful, hockey players must set both on and off-ice goals and then strive to meet them. Goals are not vague dreams but are the specific behaviors we *intend* to accomplish. In order to be achieved, dreams or wishes must be broken down and re-framed as specific goals.

SELF-TEST 2:1

1. Rate your knowledge of Goal Setting.

1	*2*	*3*	*4*	*5*
very low				*very high*

2. Rate your belief about the importance of Goal Setting.

1	*2*	*3*	*4*	*5*
very low				*very high*

3. Rate your planned use of Goal Setting.

1	*2*	*3*	*4*	*5*
very low				*very high*

To be effective, goals or objectives must be stated clearly in measurable terms, accomplished by a specific date, and subjected to evaluation and modification. Goal setting research shows goals are most successful when they are difficult and challenging, yet achievable. In a team sport, it is important that individual goals are compatible with team goals.

It is also important that outcome goals, although stated and identified, are not emphasized to the exclusion of process goals. Process goals are the "how to" aspects of goal setting. They are the strategies and procedures of how you are going to achieve specific goals. Sport psychologists Pierce and Burton (1998) found that gymnasts who set performance, process-oriented goals significantly improved their performance compared to success-oriented (outcome only) goal setters who experienced a decrease in performance. Examples of process-oriented goals in hockey are "I'm going to finish each check" or "get 5 - 8 shots on the net." Success-oriented goals in hockey are "We are going to win our next five games." That's great, but you need to focus on the specific strategies or goals of each player that will make it happen. Specific short term, intermediate, and dream goals are shown in the model provided. (See Figure 2)

This 'target approach' to goal setting is both motivating and self-reinforcing. The target can have any number of rings, and for hockey players, can be likened to a face off spot with several rings surrounding it. The face off spot, or bull's eye, is at the center (See Figure 2). The athlete is asked to identify *a dream goal* which is entered into the outer ring. Depending upon individual players, examples might be making it or staying in the NHL or on the minor league team and achieving a specific status through the season. The *seasonal goals* might be specific offense goals such as goals and assists or defensive goals such as reducing the shots by the opposition allowed on your shift or decreasing the penalty minutes you receive. The next smaller circle might be the *weekly goal* of a specific plus/minus, goal points, assist points, penalty minutes, % of face offs won, or accuracy of shots. The next ring is for practice or *game goals* which might be specific exercises on puck control and break out passes. The next ring is for *period goals* which would include specific tasks given to you by the coach for this period such as taking no penalties, being the first player to loose pucks, covering rebounds, or strategies you and your linemates have identified. Period goals can incorporate feedback from the previous period of play and can accommodate information about your opponents. The center or bulls-eye of the target model in hockey is the *shift goal.* Examples might include getting the face-off, making crisp passes, staying on-side, communicating with linemates, putting shots on the net, etc. The same model is used for each practice where the bull's eye becomes each face-off, shot, drill, pass, check, or save. You must specifically tailor individual goals for your position and must address your own specific strengths and weaknesses.

SET GOALS TO IMPROVE YOUR WEAKNESSES (Exercise 2)

There is a natural tendency for hockey players, given unstructured ice time, to practice the skills they already do best. The players with the best slap shot practice their slap shots and the best skaters practice skating drills. Players are prone to do this since these behaviors reinforce the positive self-images they desire of being good hockey players. However, realistic goal setting requires an honest appraisal of strengths and weaknesses, and then setting goals to develop the skills most in need of improvement.

TARGET MODELS AS MENTAL PREPARATION

The target model for goal setting is dynamic (changing) and can be used as part of the mental preparation process for each game. The goals of the target model are set such that the smaller, more achievable goals will gradually lead to the successful completion of the long range goals. There is a 'snowball effect' at work when you achieve even the smallest of goals, the shift goal. By focusing on your shift goal for each of the 6-8 shifts per period, you can accomplish the period goal. And by successfully stringing together three good periods, you meet the game goal. In turn, repeatedly meeting your game goals leads to the accomplishment of your seasonal and dream goals. But the dream goal can never be reached without meeting the other goals first.

Remember, even the longest journey begins with a single step!

That first step in a hockey player's journey of realizing his dream goal, of making it to the NHL, staying in the NHL, winning a Stanley Cup, being named to an All-Star team. Becoming a Regular Season 50 or 100 Point Scorer, or making it to travelling A ice hockey, you must begin with focusing on each and every shift. You must be sure that the goal set for each shift is challenging yet reachable.

The advantage of expressing goals in a measurable way is so that you can keep track of whether or not they are being achieved. Goals must be flexible and easily modified. For example, if the coach asks a player to suddenly change lines or a game plan and stress defense rather than offense, new goals must be promptly substituted into the shift, period, and game goal rings of the model. Mentally, this can be done very quickly.

SPECIFIC AND MEASURABLE GOALS

1. I will get 70% of the face-offs I take in practice and game situations in the next week.

2. I will go into the corners and take the other player's body out (when appropriate) each shift of this game.

3. I will stick handle with my head up for 15 minutes after practice each day.

4. I will get 80% of my shots on net and will look at the net as I'm shooting. To do this, I will volunteer to provide shots for the third goalie's practice.

PRE-GAME GOALS

It is not only important to set goals but also to identify the specific strategy or process goals that will help the player accomplish each goal. If you are unsure, the coach's assistance should be sought. Some coaches suggest that players set goals that relate to the physical and the mental side of the game such as in the following examples:

Physical Goals: plus/minus average, goals, assists, PPGF, PPGA, PKGF, PKGA, penalties, number of take outs, number of 1: 1 battles won, creating 2nd & 3rd efforts, limiting their 2nd & 3rd efforts, picking, driving to the net, and backchecking.

Mental Goals: rate on a scale of 1-5 your: intensity level, frequency of quality communication, concentration, ability to stay pumped up, and your ability to recover from a bad shift or a bad period. Set goals to improve the self-rating scores that are low. Mental goals must be set to deal with the terrific ups and downs associated with competitive hockey.

The rollercoaster ride of being on top then on the bottom, of playing on a first line one period, benched the next and/or not dressed for the next game, stresses the coping resources of even the most mentally tough! Recognizing that it is a game of change and then setting goals to help *stay* on an even keel is important. Sometimes players don't really understand hockey. They automatically think the first line is the best line. It isn't always. The year I worked in the NHL, two fourth-line players were signed first to ensure their defensive forward roles. Many USHL, college, and high school hockey players (and often their parents) are so mentally fragile they assume it's a big demotion; they sulk and turn what could be a powerful weapon into an embarrassment because of their unwillingness to deliver what's best for the team.

SELF-EVALUATION (Exercise 3)

You should review game films and elicit feedback at the end of the week from your coaching staff to ensure that your goals are being met. When goals are expressed in desired percentages, frequencies per shift, period, game, and per week, an evaluation of your success in achieving your goals is possible. Significant others can help provide objective feedback that is constructive and helpful rather than anecdotal criticism which can hinder a player. Complete Exercise 3 after each practice and game.

GOAL SETTING IN THE NHL (Exercise 4 - Mental Log Book)

Phil Esposito, center for the New York Rangers, used to keep a 'mental book' on the defensemen he played against, noting the direction each turned best. He could then capitalize on their weaknesses. He thought defensemen should keep a book of the strengths, weaknesses, and tendencies of opposing forwards, and that goaltenders should keep a log of opposing forwards and defensemen. Phil Esposito's use of a mental book reveals the mental preparation and mental rehearsal that takes place in the NHL by some of the top players.

Steve Yzerman commented on the importance of concentrating and improving every time you are on the ice. This means that it does not help to go through practices or workouts by just passively going through the motions. It is said of one of the greatest hockey players the game has ever known, "Wayne Gretzky attributes much of his success to his ability to set *meaningful* goals, to maintain a minute-to-minute focus during play, and to have fun as he performs."[14] Brett Hull set a specific goal of making a certain number of points per game a few seasons ago, and was successful in achieving them in spite of considerable pressure, a large contract, media attention, and having forwards assigned to shadow him throughout a game. He enjoyed the big thrill and pay-off in the spring of 1999 when his goal in the third overtime period in the Stanley Cup was allowed!

Rule: Make it a rule to never put your skates on without having a plan for what you want to accomplish that game or practice.

<u>Figure 2</u> Examples of Target Goal Setting

<u>Table
1.</u>

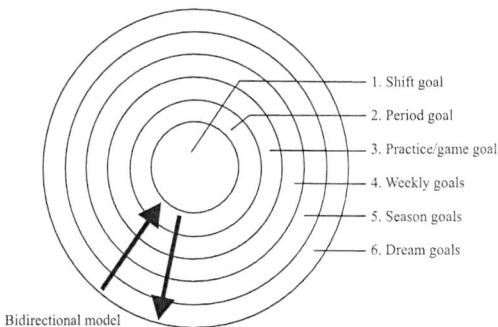

Bidirectional model

1. Shift goal
2. Period goal
3. Practice/game goal
4. Weekly goals
5. Season goals
6. Dream goals

---

[14] Loehr, J. E. Ibid. p. 78

Examples of Specific Goals for Each Player Position (ideas, only)

1. Shift Goals
Forwards

-head up
-staying onside
-tenacious
-crashing the net
-sticks on ice
-forecheck

1. Shift Goals
Defense

-take the body
-eye on chest of attacker
-stick extended
-pinch to center
-crisp break out
-clear out front

1. Shift Goals
Goal Tenders

-concentration with relaxation
-positive self-talk
-stay involved
-make forward commit
-play angle
-stretch between shifts

2. Period Goals
Forwards

-strong defense
-back checking
- (+/-) for the line
-no penalties
-lead the skater

2. Period Goals
Defense

-patience
-make shooter commit
-positive self-talk
-no retaliation penalties
-communicate

2. Period Goals
Goal Tenders

-play one shot at a time
-"stay in the moment"
(avoid looking ahead or behind)
-aggressive in the crease
-passing

3. Game/ Practice Goals
Forwards

-consistency
-get 70% face offs
-into corners after puck
-see open net-then shoot

3. Game/Practice Goals
Defense

-slap shots 90% low
-hard, effective checks
-don't give up our zone
-tie up in front of net

3. Game/Practice Goals
Goal Tenders

% GA
-head in the game
-hold the short side
-close 5 hole

4. Weekly Goals

You can evaluate if you are on target to realize season goals such as total points, goals/assists. Reset new goals if some have been mastered and keep challenging yourself. See what has been accomplished, reward yourself, then set harder goals and state the strategies to meet them. Keep your goals consistent with the team's goals and the expectations you and the coach agreed upon for your role.

5. Season Goals

Season goals can be modified as week-by-week progress toward the season goal is assessed. Modifications can be made as needed. Injuries, coaching, or team roster changes may necessitate a change in goals. Appropriate assistance is sought from coaches, teammates, and when necessary, sports science counselors, etc.

6. Dream Goals

You must identify and state your dream goals at the outset. Then, you must work diligently through the other goals of the target model if you hope to achieve your long-range, dream goals.

BENEFITS OF GOAL SETTING

An important benefit of goal setting is that it helps you distinguish between what you can and what you cannot control. As goals are realized, you will become more confident and begin to take pride in personal accomplishments regardless of a game's outcome. For example, Mario Lemieux earned recognition despite playing for a team unable to win. Finally, Lemieux's team, Pittsburgh, claimed the Stanley Cup in 1991 under his on-ice leadership and the off-ice coaching of "Badger" Bob Johnson.

Players who successfully remain in the NHL for several years continuously set increasingly challenging fitness and performance goals. Players like Igor Larianov, Paul Kariya, Steve Yzerman, and Shjon Podein also work on goal setting during both the competitive and the increasingly short off season.

INDIVIDUAL GOALS MUST BE IN HARMONY WITH TEAM GOALS

Because hockey is a team sport, individual goals must be compatible with team goals. Teamwork and the sacrificing of one's personal goals are almost always required of the individual player to some extent. The flexible player resets the areas he identifies for improvement to ensure compatibility with the goals of the team. Remember, hockey has a scoring system which pays equal tribute to skill and effort: *scoring both a goal and an assist have the same value, one point.* Working with your coach and communicating with linemates may help clarify specific goals that need to be addressed by you, by the line, and by the team. Goal setting helps promote a good work ethic which is necessary if your dreams and your team's dreams are to be realized. No strategy used in sport psychology is more powerful than Goal Setting. Darryl Sittler, captain of the Toronto Maple Leafs many years ago, stated, "I fully believe that writing something (your goals) down means you will give it more thought than if you had just said it."[15]

And Step by Step Since Time Began, I See the Steady Gain of Man

---

[15] Sittler, D. Ibid.

Exercise 2 (Setting Your Own Goals- use pencil and erase for each game)

Complete One of These Before Each Practice and Game

Target Goal Setting

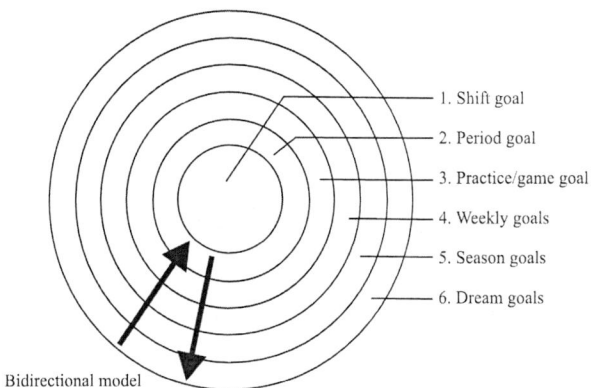

- 1. Shift goal
- 2. Period goal
- 3. Practice/game goal
- 4. Weekly goals
- 5. Season goals
- 6. Dream goals

Bidirectional model

1. Shift by Shift Goals   2. Period Goals   3. Practice/Game Goals

_____ _____ _____

_____ _____ _____

_____ _____ _____

4. Weekly Goals   5. Season Goals   6. Dream Goals

_____ _____ _____

_____ _____ _____

_____ _____ _____

Exercise 3 - Self Evaluation of Performance - After Each Practice or Game

1. How successful was I in meeting my goals?
    Not at all   1   2   3   4   5   6   7   Extremely Successful

2. How motivated was I for the practice or the game?
    Not at all   1   2   3   4   5   6   7   Extremely Successful

3. How energized was I for the practice or the game?
    Not at all   1   2   3   4   5   6   7   Extremely Successful

4. Were there any self-statements or events that either helped or hindered
    your performance? If yes, what were they? _____
    _____
    _____
    _____
    _

5. Identify the strategies you will use for the next practice or game to
    improve and learn from this one? _____
    _____
    _____
    _____

Exercise 4 - A Mental Log Book on the Opposing Team

Opposing Team _____ Date_____ Home or Away _____

Players	Strengths	Weaknesses	Plan to Counter

An example of concrete goal setting in sport is the
Career Best Effort program which Pat Riley instituted with

the Los Angeles Lakers and the New York Knicks, the 1994 NBA Champions. He described this system in his book, "The Winner Within". The Career Best Effort program involved comparing team members to themselves and to players on opposing teams with similar positions and role definitions. It helped individuals and the team rise to new levels of performance. It measured effort as well as points, rebounds, and assists. Coach Riley claims the system does not work without the players', coaches', and trainers' input and enthusiasm. It required a total team effort. Most hockey teams at all levels establish their team goals at the outset of the season and strive for a total team effort.

Many NHL professional franchises, national, and Division I college teams have access to computerized statistical programs that rapidly graph and display such specifics as shots on net, passes, number of checks, forechecks, etc. Such software (i.e., developed by Tom Aney) provides both coaches and players with information between periods on which to base their next period and shift goals.

"The game is won on the ice - not at home or in the locker room" (Bertanga, 1990). Nevertheless, "opportunity comes to the prepared mind," and goal setting is an important component of good mental preparation which, like good physical conditioning, permits a player to take to the ice, in a state of positive anticipation and respectful confidence.

SELF-TEST 2: 2

1. Rate your knowledge of Goal Setting.

1	*2*	*3*	*4*	*5*
very low				*very high*

2. Rate your belief about the importance of Goal Setting.

1	*2*	*3*	*4*	*5*
very low				*very high*

3. Rate your planned use of Goal Setting.

1	*2*	*3*	*4*	*5*
very low				*very high*

The best kind of pride is that which compels a man to do his very best work, even if no one is watching!

Games are won and lost as a result of the goals set
and achieved during practice when the stands are empty.
Reprinted with permission of USA Hockey

6

COMPETITION REFLECTIONS AND MENTAL PREPARATION PLANS

Begin Where You Are But Don't Stay Where You Are

Sport psychologists such as Dr. Terry Orlick (University of Ottawa) believe that an ideal starting point for the athlete who wishes to become mentally tough is to identify dream and seasonal goals. The next task is to identify what specific physical and mental skills need to be worked on and what strategies must be learned if the goals are to be realized. We have used aspects of Dr. Orlick's method with a Junior A USHL team for years.

SELF-TEST 3:1

1. Rate your knowledge of Mental Preparation Plans.

1	*2*	*3*	*4*	*5*
very low				*very high*

2. Rate your belief about the importance of Mental Preparation Plans.

1	*2*	*3*	*4*	*5*
very low				*very high*

3. Rate your planned use of Mental Preparation Plans.

1	*2*	*3*	*4*	*5*
very low				*very high*

COMPETITION REFLECTIONS (Exercise 5)

The suggested format for Goal Assessment, Reflections On Best Game Ever, Worst Game Ever, Development of a Mental and Physical Preparation Plan (Content and Sequence), a Competition Reflections Plan, and a Refocusing plan as they might have been suggested by Orlick have been adapted for hockey.[16]

BEST PERFORMANCE REFLECTION

It is important that you look back on your *best hockey performance ever,* recalling all of the minor details that may have influenced your play. Such reflections may include pre-game details such as listening to music, a favorite meal, a coaching pep talk, your level of pre-game anxiety, your level of arousal during the game, and the importance of the game. These should be recorded under appropriate headings as to whether they were physical or psychological factors that helped to produce the best performance. By recalling the best performance in minute detail, you can learn how to repeat the steps necessary to reach your best performance again.

WORST PERFORMANCE REFLECTION

The worst performance must also be recalled and the details recorded. The purpose of making you go through these memories is so that worst performances may be avoided in the future. You must identify problems with girlfriends or wives, intimidation from the opposition, bad practices, critical comments from teammates, coaches, or the media, fear of injury, re-injury, or other factors which might have negatively affected your athletic performance. Recent illness, negative

[16] Orlick, T. *Psyching for sport: Mental training for athletes.* (Leisure Press: Champaign, IL. 1986)

self-talk, superstitions that backfired, lack of faith in the skate sharpening person, a dislike of the new sticks, or adjustment to a new team or line are also concerns that may be included in the record of worst performances.

PREPARING THE PERSONAL PREPARATION PLAN

After the best and worst competition reflections are recorded, the next step is to compare the two lists. The mental preparation plan is the result of all physical and psychological factors believed to enhance or facilitate performance (which are included or retained) while all factors believed to negatively effect performance are excluded. If eliminating these negative factors is not possible, a short list of these factors should be made. Intimidation by defensemen on another team or discomfort with new sticks, gloves, or goalie pads are examples of factors which may not be entirely eliminated. However, make sure to include them because, although the ultimate goal is to have a positive but realistic mental preparation plan, strategies can be introduced to help change your attitude toward some of these unavoidable aspects of the game. For example, strategies such as watching game tapes and talking to the coach about "how to play against" a specific intimidating defenseman (play to the player's weakness) can be helpful. Also, ordering sticks in time to allow several practices before important games permits an adjustment period. Now you can examine the list and identify strategies that you can use to deal with the factors that enhance or hinder performance.

MENTAL PLAN CONTENT AND SEQUENCE CONTENT

You must order all of the desirable pre-game factors and events in a sequence that you are prepared to follow before each game. For example, make a list of all the food choices for pre-game meals, the amount of stretching needed, the taping of sticks, and the length of time needed to listen to mental preparation tapes, working on goal sheets, and order of equipment dress.

Sequence: The *sequence* columns are where you list the times and organize the content into the order in which you want your routine. A sequence might start with the evening meal the night before the game and would include the previous night's activities such as preparing and reading your mental book on the strengths and weaknesses of opposing players, a session of relaxation and positive directed imagery focused on the team to be played, an inspiring movie, and a specified bed-time. The number of hours of sleep, breakfast, arrival at the rink, relaxation and imagery routine, optimum minutes of stretching, dressing routine, and psych up time would also be included in the sequence or routine. When you have prepared a sequence or pre-game routine, it will increase your sense of preparedness and reassure you that all of the things that are within your control are, in fact, under control.

One player I worked with for two years was a capable defensemen who took his mental preparation seriously. He prepared the same way for every game. He liked to arrive at the arena early for a game and sit alone in the stands getting himself into the ideal mental state and visually rehearsing defensive plays. He became known for his consistency and his absence of mental errors, which earned him a Division I scholarship.

SUPERSTITIONS AND RITUALS

A word is needed here about superstitions and rituals which are used in an attempt to control the 'luck square' of the attribution theory model and bring a player to ideal performance. Hockey players have a wide variety of superstitions and rituals. Examples are: dressing in a certain order, wearing one side of a jersey tucked in, being the first on the ice, or the last, needing to score before leaving the ice during warm-up, and banging the goal posts in a specific sequence. Some players, after their team has been on a winning streak, will refuse to wash team jerseys, shave, cut hair, or replace broken equipment. Gretzky had a torn jock strap that he couldn't do without!

Most of the superstitions or rituals I have listed are fine, but since we have the ability to believe what we want to believe, it is puzzling that some hockey players allow themselves to be convinced that something they can't control can have the 'power' to determine their performance or fate. Why, after years of practice and developing abilities at great expense, should a player let go of 'control' and become a pawn of fate?

However, hockey players aren't the only ones who often let superstitions effect their performances. One example of 'letting go of control' happened to a young figure skater I worked with. Despite practicing for 8 hours a day and years of living separated from her family to be near a specific coach, she confided she could skate a good performance only if her coach held her gloves. Last minute frantic searches for her coach and fears that her coach would be late almost undid her, leaving her totally unable to concentrate on mentally rehearsing her program prior to her competition. When she understood what she was doing to herself, she was able to 'let go' of this superstition and substitute 'rituals' which she believed were lucky but, more importantly, were under her control. A certain way of setting her gloves in her locker, an order of dressing, or listening to a lucky song on her tape deck began to provide her with a sense of control. Similarly, hockey players must focus upon the things that they can control and learn to accept those that they cannot.

Ken Dryden, goaltender with the Montreal Canadians

and five time winner of the Vezina trophy for the best NHL goal tender, had several irrational superstitions. He stated, "I must take the first shot, it must strike the boards to the right of my net between the protective glass and the ice. If it doesn't, I will play poorly. So, as the team waits anxiously, I look for an opening, 15-20 feet of uncrowded space to take my important shot."[17] Why should shooting the puck against the boards once before a game have any effect on performance during an entire game'? Players need to recognize that such irrational superstitions are only in their heads. But if it is in your head, then you can control it, rather than letting it control you!

Dryden also used to look for Joyce, a Montreal Forum usherette, behind the visiting team's bench. After a conversation with Joyce before one game the team happened to win. He began a ritual in which he would smile and nod to Joyce for luck. Once the team started losing, he stopped doing this and never spoke to Joyce again. Poor confused Joyce! Talk about a senseless self-fulfilling prophecy. He went on in his book, *The Game,* to add: "It's one of the many superstitions I've come to burden myself with. I don't tell anyone about them, I'm not proud of them, I know I should be strong enough to decide to no longer be a prisoner to them." Ken Dryden was a very successful goalie, one of the best in the game! One can only wonder how many more shots he could have stopped, had he not been giving up so much control. Dryden writes honestly and played the game before we understood some of the negative effects of adopting rituals and superstitions that are out of our control. *Players of today can avoid getting into the same traps!*

When I work with players, I advise them to *keep their rituals* which provide details for mental absorption and concentration but to believe in and select 'luck objects or behaviors' that they can control. From my viewpoint, some of

---

[17] Dryden, Ken. *The Game.* (Penguin Books: New York, NY. 1983) p. 177.

their beliefs still seem irrational, but once they understand the principle of not giving up the power they have worked so hard to achieve, I think the rituals they choose for themselves are better. It is important for hockey players to keep their power and not to undermine themselves mentally.

There is no one luckier than he who thinks himself so
– German Proverb

COMPETITION EVALUATION PLAN

Once your mental preparation plan is developed and your rituals are under control, a competition evaluation form is used. This form gives you an opportunity to reflect on your performances in order to determine which part of your preparation plan was effective and which part was not. The pre-competition and competition plans are then modified to include new strategies and content which is either added or deleted after objective consideration. The result of this process is the revised plan which then serves as the preparation plan for the next game. As the personal plan undergoes revision it begins to stabilize until, eventually, it requires few changes. Consistency in preparation promotes consistency in performance.

BENEFITS OF MENTAL PREPARATION PLANS

Individualized mental preparation plans provide a sense of control and reassurance that all that can be done, has been done. This provides a positive focus for constructive thoughts. The brain occupied in this manner has little time to be concerned with negative thoughts or fears. Successful performances are expected, which then develop into a self-fulfilling prophecy. In the event that a player does not succeed, the competition evaluation plan also serves as a constructive learning tool. The player can determine why he failed to perform up to expectations and then make the necessary corrections.

REFOCUSING DURING COMPETITION

The goal of the ideal mental focus in sport is 'to be all there, in the moment'. This is a difficult concept because we frequently separate mental and physical performance. How many times do we go for a walk, a run, a sail, a canoe trip, or a drive and while our body is performing one skill, our mind is totally off, on a different track? The high performance athlete can't do that during a game. A competitive hockey player must reconnect the mind-body flow so he is all there and in control of the experience. The hockey player must be *totally* on the ice and *in each shift* with both mind and body. When other thoughts distract and remove the athlete's mind from the moment... the flow is interrupted. The faster the athlete realizes he has mentally taken himself out of the game, and gets refocused, the better his performance will be. Dr. Terry Orlick suggests that athletes develop a plan which has cue words such as STOP, DEEP BREATH, REFOCUS, POSITIVE ENERGY, FLOW. Hockey players need a way to consistently detect a loss of concentration, stop the drift, and rapidly get their heads back into the game. (Channel Clicking is discussed in Chapter 8 and can be the cue to rapidly switching back into the focus or flow.) This is what is meant when Gretzky claims he "maintains a moment-to-moment focus." Maintaining focus is important but so is recognizing when it is lost and having a plan to reacquire your concentration. The goal in hockey is to be playing with a feeling of 'automaticity' or flow. Unfortunately, this flow state is often interrupted by thoughts of significant others, of how they might be evaluating the player's performance, or by the presence of scouts, bad penalties, or a remark from a linemate or a coach. Being hooked, tripped, or having an opponent make inflammatory remarks are often deliberate attempts to mentally take you out of the game. Don't let yourself be mentally drawn offside.

The Most Important Thing is to Learn to Rule Oneself
- Von Goethe

DEALING WITH THE MEDIA

I have thoughts on this subject which are not yet supported by research, but are based on experience and from watching the influence of the media on the careers of hockey players over the years. I favor the approach Herb Brooks took with the 1980 'Miracle on Ice' team when he restricted player interviews prior to the Olympics and controlled all press releases. The benefits to team cohesion of not allowing a few stars to get all the attention cannot be underestimated. Bob Johnson may have had that in mind when his Pittsburgh Penguins did not attend a press conference in Minneapolis during the Stanley Cup playoffs in 1991, a series in which they came from behind to win. After the Montreal Canadiens were interviewed following their Stanley Cup win over LA in 1993, Brian Bellows was asked how he would compare the Canadiens and North Stars organizations. Bellows spoke about the depth of the Canadiens organization and how the pressure and expectations of the players were distributed throughout the team. When he was with the North Stars he felt that enormous pressure by the organization and media was placed on the shoulders of just a few players, which seemed to interfere with teamwork and success. When I see just a few hockey players on a team receive 'ink', I often see a decrement in the performance of those players. Whether they become overconfident or less motivated because some of their drives are satisfied (Chapter 11), whether teammates who are jealous may fail to deliver the perfect pass or fail to protect the net with quite the same intensity, I am not sure. Media attention is certainly flattering and boosts the individual ego but it is also a distraction. I believe it disrupts a player's flow and consequently the performance suffers. On the other hand, some players such as Ray Bourke, Dominique Hasek, Peter Forsberg, John LeClair, Joe Sakic, and Steve Yzerman seem to have taken 'fame' in stride and, like Wayne Gretzky and Jaromir Jagr, have not experienced a drop in performance. I think these professionals are so sincerely committed to seeing their team enjoy success that they are unaffected by media attention.

Although the players mentioned seem mature in their attitudes, personal needs or drives are more often an influence in determining sport performance than people realize. I often chuckle about the baseball player who was being jeered by the fans for errors he didn't believe were his fault. Finally, he thought, "if you really want to see me when I commit an error, watch this". Instead of throwing the ball to home plate, he deliberately threw it into the stands! How would you feel if one of your teammates disrupted your important game by blowing up and throwing a puck into the stands?

Most people enjoy recognition and attention and like to be rewarded for their performances. Athletes are no different. But a team game requires that all players be pulling in the same direction. When one or two players become the darlings of the media, jealousies arise and noses get out of joint. The hard workers in hockey may take a terrific physical beating night after night and still be regularly ignored by the press while the skill players receive all the media attention. Friction develops among players which can undermine the team unity or cohesion. The same thing happens when coaching comments to the press stress the play of a few select individuals. It must have been an extremely unifying season for the Dallas Stars to see their franchise players Mike

Modano and Brett Hull playing consistently on both ends of the ice. Similarly, Mike Pecca for the Buffalo Sabres is a skilled offensive player, but he's clearly earned the respect of his teammates and coaches because of his willingness to do whatever it takes to move the puck into scoring position.

Michael Jordan recognized the need for equity and insisted that his whole team be allowed to make a video with him to promote Disney World. Apparently, he was asked to make the video alone but instead he asked if the Chicago Bulls could appear together. This created a unifying rather than disruptive experience for his team.

Ideally, coaches and captains should strive to see that, when possible, team members receive or are offered parity in media attention. Because of player differences, some players prefer to avoid the media while others enjoy it and seek it out. Furthermore, members of the media, general managers, and team publicity personnel also have their own agendas and ideas of what and who "will sell". It is important that this potential conflict or threat to team unity be discussed up front before it becomes a problem. More importantly, I believe *that a coach's criticism of players should be private and not released to the press.* Apparently, players liked Coach Roger Neilson because "he didn't just stand and scream, he discussed hockey and coaching theory and encouraged us to contribute our ideas." According to Sittler and Salming, "When Roger Neilson was coaching, guys came to play every night." When a player is publicly criticized, it embarrasses the player and can destroy that player's loyalty to the coach. Any trust bond that existed between the player and the coach can be immediately destroyed by public humiliation. It also drives away fans and undermines their confidence in the team. Players need to be equally cautious about making critical statements to the media about their teammates or coach. Public criticism can pull a team apart and impair fan's ability to identify with the team.

Most teams need and want media attention to help generate ticket sales. A wise coach tries to ensure that recognition for the team effort be spread out among the players. The few players who are identified as stars early, are wise to keep their comments brief, be generous to their teammates, and not take the fickle recognition they are receiving too seriously. In hockey, a cliche, which I don't fully accept but in this context has merit, is 'there is no I in team'. (We put an I in team in Chapter 10.)

The only praise that is damaging is that which we allow ourselves to believe

DEALING WITH PARENTS AND SIGNIFICANT OTHERS

As outlined in the introduction, hockey today is not the same game it was during the Stanley Cup in 1903. In those days, kids played for hours on neighborhood rinks and frozen ponds and were away from the scrutiny and continuous evaluation of coaches and significant others. It was okay to try new things, to 'dipsy doodle', to try new moves, to succeed, to fail, to take risks, to laugh, to have fun, and to find joy in the game. Today however, kids usually learn the game skating in indoor arenas and hockey schools where they are subjected to constant evaluation. Much of this is positive because the learning opportunities are enormous but there are also drawbacks of which we should be mindful.

PARENTAL PRESSURE

As one sport psychologist stated "parents have climbed into the blood streams of their children."[18] While parents may love their children and believe they are doing what is best, many attempt to create a star hockey player,

---

[18] Ogilvie, Bruce. *"What Price Glory?"* videotape CBS

making great sacrifices of money and time to support the player in summer hockey schools. They spend their winter on the road with traveling teams so their child can gain experience in tournaments against better competition. As a consequence of parental involvement, the child's performance is measured against the parent's standards and expectations. The weekend of traveling may be judged a success or failure on the basis of whether or not the youngster put the puck in the net or failed to keep it out, depending on his position. Hockey players often carry the burden of their parent's (spoken or unspoken) expectation that a scholarship or 'family bragging rights' is the pay back for their sacrifices. A recent study we did (with Jena Berryman) of three southern Minnesota high school varsity teams showed that, on average, these players traveled for 5.66 years before playing high school hockey! This is no small sacrifice of time and money by players, parents, and coaches. Hockey players need to get in touch with what it is that they themselves want to gain by playing the game. Then they can set their own goals and measure their performance against their own standards. Hockey performance will not be optimal if the player is burdened by parents' and loved ones' expectations. This is a major challenge for today's athletes. Well intentioned parents who have never played are often living vicariously through their child's experience. Significant others, who never played or who no longer participate in sport may not understand the demands of the game and the reality of the opponents' skill. Playing at your best does not always guarantee success in terms of game outcome. Parents who are actively involved in some of their own exercise or sporting events seem to understand the pressures that their child may be going through. By understanding sports, parents can lessen the pressure and help free the player of the burden of others' expectations.

While it is important to be free of *unrealistic expectations,* we are not talking about evading *realistic expectations* that the coach and teammates may have of the player. Sometimes players feel weighted down with unrealistic expectations which may feel like you are skating with a knapsack full of sand or weights. The principle of freeing yourself from others' expectations is illustrated in Exercise 6.

<u>Get the Monkey off Your Back</u> (Exercise 6)

One sport psychologist demonstrated this principle in an exercise by having one player jump onto the shoulders of another. Then he asked, "How far and how fast can you skate and play with that monkey on your back? Get rid of it and do what you want to do for you, because you want it."

Perhaps an interesting example of this was Jim Craig, the Olympic goaltender who was in net when the Americans clinched the gold in 1980. Instead of celebrating with his teammates who skated into a huge pile of euphoric bodies to hug each other, Jim skated into center ice and stood alone scanning the crowd for his father. His mother had died and he had played to win as a tribute to her memory. I found that sight alarming and it haunted me for a long time after. I think his mother's memory and possibly pledges to his father that he'd win this for mom, were monkeys on his back. I fear those issues were not resolved when he was whisked off to try his hand in the NHL.

By contrast, let us look at Bill Johnson, a U.S. downhill ski racer who also won an Olympic gold medal. During an interview he was asked, "How do you feel about winning a gold for the United States?" He looked at the reporter incredulously and said, "For the United States, are you kidding? I did this for Bill Johnson." This is perhaps one of the healthiest mental attitudes one can have in sport. After all, the United States did not practice with him on cold nights, hit trees, break legs, tear knees, or face the fear and pain he must have experienced. It was Bill Johnson that worked hard, for Bill Johnson's sake and he alone should share in his own reward. The people of the United States may have the right to be proud of one of their Olympic competitors but one must not confuse the responsibilities and rewards of competitors with spectators. In other words, Bill Johnson did not carry the monkey of the United States' expectations on his back and as a reduction of this pressure, he may have been able to perform at his best and win the medal. If you really want to be good at hockey, you must want it for yourself. It must be important to you or else you won't be hungry for it. When hockey players feel free of the added weight of others' unrealistic expectations, they will perform more often in an ideal performance state.

JOY OF THE GAME

Hockey players at all levels are most motivated by a pure enjoyment of the game. When mites and squirts play the game, it is all they can do to keep from falling down. They come off the ice at the end of a game, tired, sweaty, and happy. Often they aren't sure what the score was, or even who won but they had fun chasing the puck around and trying to score. Perhaps Gretzky said it best when he said, "We get paid millions of dollars to do our best in the NHL, but we play in the Canada Cup for the love of the game. When you do it for those reasons, and you play the hardest and the best hockey of your life, the payoff seems pure and lasting and unforgettable."[19] Any player who has played the game at any competitive level usually understands Gretzky's love of the game.

[19] Gretzky, Wayne. *An Autobiography.* (Harper Collins Publishers: New York, NY. 1990) p.161.

Athletes working on their mental preparation plans need to adjust the level of contact with parents, girlfriends, and significant others based on the power these persons have in influencing their performances. Decisions about whether or not to make contact with significant others may have to be explained to these well intentioned but sometimes overly involved persons.

As a parent in the days before I was a student of sport psychology, I can remember watching my 6 foot, 185 pound defensemen son, listening to music before a game necessary to win before advancing to the Minnesota state high school hockey tournament. I asked if he was really 'up' for the game and excited enough? I must have been daft. I know now that I should have left him alone, taught him a relaxation skill, or suggested a quiet walk. A player needing a butterfly net to catch the butterflies in his stomach doesn't need to receive more pressure from his mom or anyone else. Although some players need to get really "psyched up" for games, he was not that type. As with many good athletes, he overcame my intrusions on his mental preparation and played well through his high school career in spite of his mother's well meaning over-parenting. Perhaps I would have been in the 'content column' of his mental preparation plan as a person to avoid on game day.

True success is overcoming the fear of being unsuccessful
- Paul Sweeney

DEALING WITH THE COACH

Some coaches have a positive influence and others a negative effect on their hockey players' mental preparation. Because mental preparation is so individual, what is positive for 30% of the team may be neutral for 40% and be detrimental for 30%. Incidentally, this is the breakdown of the usefulness most hockey players find with a mental toughness program. The Junior team who won 2 National Championships rated their mental toughness program with those same percentages: 1/3 finding it extremely helpful, 1/3 finding it somewhat helpful, and 1/3 finding it of little help. Therefore, a coach who pumps his team up will provide inspiration to some yet push others, who are trying to calm themselves down, over the optimal edge. A coach who is too laid back may not be able to supply the intensity which under-aroused players prefer but might be better suited for players who get too psyched up. It is important for athletes to learn to control themselves and take the responsibility of setting and keeping their own internal thermostats to ensure ideal performance.

For a man to conquer himself is the first and noblest of all victories - Plato.

To do this, you must learn to 'separate the wheat from the chaff, keep the kernel, and throw the rest away'. Although you must listen to the wisdom, facts, and strategies which the coach might explain, you must also insulate yourself from the emotion attached to these words if it will have a negative influence on your performance. Sometimes coaches are under pressure to win from the franchise or they may have their own personal agenda. The 'we-must-win-tonight' speech might place too much pressure on the player who needs to be free to take risks, to make the big plays. Other laid back players might need the intensity and will accept and benefit from the extra pressure. The point I am trying to make here is that there is no perfect coaching strategy which will help every single player on the team. Instead, you must set your own goals, develop your game preparation plans, maintain your focus, refocus when necessary and when appropriate, insulate yourself from carrying anyone or anything on your back if it will interfere with optimal performance. This is a requirement for success for the individual player and leads to success for the team.

ADDING PRESSURE DOESN'T HELP

As a ski patroller, I would find it difficult to bring an injured skier down a steep hill on a toboggan if I began to add pressure on myself in this already tense situation. Suppose I start to add the pressure that the victim is the ski area's owner, or a lawyer who specializes in negligence law suits. How steady do you think my hands on the toboggan and my legs upon the snow would be if I am so stressed out I can hardly think?

This principle works the same in life as well as in sport. A surgeon won't operate any better because the patient is the President of the United States. In fact, the added pressure of knowing who his patient is may make his hands tremble. And pilots don't land planes any better when they are being observed and tested on their landing procedures. Most motor skills are executed optimally when the person who needs to execute the skill is free to concentrate, to be in the moment, and to react to the specific situation undistracted by additional stresses.

If a problem between a hockey player and the coach is major, good communication is essential. The athlete should document the kinds of remarks he responds to most positively before and after games and discuss these in a pre-arranged meeting with the coach. The coach can review the player's needs and avoid remarks that are devastating to that player's performance confidence. However, players need to remember that a coach has many players and details to focus on. Mental preparation is the player's own responsibility. It's up to the players to keep their heads in the game!

In conclusion, mental preparation plans are based on competition reflection and take time to develop. Players who take the time and make the effort usually have favorable results. The players (1/3) who rated their mental toughness programs most highly were clearly in the group finding success with their hockey careers. Many players I have worked with have received scholarships, made college teams, made it to the National tryouts, and to the NHL.

This book does not seek to minimize the importance *of* physical talent for without it the player cannot advance! However, there are many players who have talent but when they add the performance enhancement that comes with mental toughness and mental preparation, they become an athletic force to be reckoned with. Mental toughness can be developed but it takes patience.

Perfection is attained by slow degrees; it requires the hand of time - Voltaire

Exercise 5

Competition Reflections

The purpose of the competition reflections exercise is to identify factors conducive to your best and worst performances. Once these factors are defined, it is easy to become directed toward performance enhancement. Then, goals can be identified using the target model (page 42).

Best Performance Reflections- Why?, When?, Where?

_____

_____

_____

_____

Worst Performance Reflections- Why?, When?, Where?

_____

_____

_____

_____

_____

Mental Preparation Plan
(Complete in pencil-so you can rework before each game)

Content: All the things physical and psycho-social you want included- evening before a game, game day, warm up, game.

_____

_____

_____

Mental Preparation Plan
(Complete in pencil-so you can rework before each game)

Sequence:

Evening–Before Game Day–Locker Room/Warm Up–Game–Refocus

_____

_____

_____

Competition Reflections

What worked today or tonight'? What do I need to change?

_____

_____

_____

Work these factors into your mental preparation plan for the next game. Incorporate them into the mental logbook along with your goal setting.

Exercise 6- Get the Monkey off Your Back

In a team setting, match up with partners and carry your partner: He or she is the monkey on your back.[20] Walk 10-15 feet. Think of 'your monkey' as the burden of 'unrealistic expectations', the way you feel when you place too many 'shoulds' on yourself. <u>Achievable</u> goals never feel as heavy as the <u>vague</u> shoulds and musts. After you release your partner, remember the feeling of weight and the difference when the weight is off your back. Commit to a season free of *unrealistic burdens*. Then switch partners and repeat the exercise.

SELF-TEST 3: 2

1. Rate your knowledge of Mental Preparation Plans.

1	*2*	*3*	*4*	*5*
very low				*very high*

2. Rate your belief about the importance of Mental Preparation Plans.

1	*2*	*3*	*4*	*5*
very low				*very high*

3. Rate your planned use of Mental Preparation Plans.

1	*2*	*3*	*4*	*5*
very low				*very high*

---

[20] Orlick T., Ravizza K., Rotella R. *Demonstration at Canadian Association of Sport Services,* Montreal, Que, 1989.

The U.S. Jr. National Team (1991) prepares for "Monkey
on Your Back"
Reprinted with permission of USA Hockey

7

AROUSAL LEVEL AND OPTIMAL FLOW ZONE

According to eminent sport psychologist Ranier Martens, psychological stress has robbed more athletes of physical energy, victory, and enjoyment in sport than any other factor. Hockey players are no exception. As the importance of winning becomes increasingly emphasized in competitive sports, the pressure and anxiety of performing well will increase accordingly. The problem of helping athletes prepare for competition is more often one of calming them down rather than psyching them up, as is widely believed. In surveys of major college teams, over 40% of the athletes reported pre-performance anxiety which they believed interfered with their effectiveness.[21]

SELF-TEST 4:1

1. Rate your knowledge of Arousal Level and the Optimal Flow Zone.

1	2	3	4	5
very low				*very high*

2. Rate your belief about the importance of Arousal Level and the Optimal Flow Zone.

1	2	3	4	5
very low				*very high*

3. Rate your planned use of Arousal Level and the Optimal Flow Zone.

1	2	3	4	5
very low				*very high*

---

[21] Martens, Ranier. *Coaches Guide to Sport Psychology.* (Human Kinetics: Champaign IL. 1987)

Stress can lead athletes to believe they are incompetent, deny them the opportunity of demonstrating the skills they have mastered in practice, and may lead to conflict, injury, and burnout. Stress occurs when there is an imbalance between the demands on a player and the player's perceived capabilities. Stress has three elements: (a) your environment, (b) your beliefs, and (c) your response in the form of arousal (the activation of the mind and body). Most athletes tend to believe the stress they experience is caused by their environment. A player may think such things as, "The coach kept putting on the pressure, my Dad said we needed to win, there were so many people and scouts, I panicked." These are examples of blaming the environment.

Our beliefs, or perceptions, are important to our interpretation of the level of stress we experience. One athlete, in seeing a hockey arena packed with people might think, "it's a great opportunity for me to show what I can do," while another might think, "how embarrassing it will be if I make a mistake in front of all those people." The same arena filled with the same number of people but one hockey player views the situation positively and the other negatively. Some stress is necessary before a game. The game of hockey requires intensity and a high level of energy. This game can only be played well if players get a little excited and charged up. However, the athlete is always the best judge of how much stress is optimal for him. The term *arousal* refers to the mental, physiological, and behavioral responses of the hockey player to stress. The following Table shows some of the physiological, mental, and behavioral symptoms of stress that hockey players might experience.

Symptoms of Stress

Physiological	Mental	Behavioral
Increased heart rate and blood pressure	Worry, tension	Rapid talking
Increased sweating	Feeling overwhelmed	Foot tapping

Increased pupil dilation	Inability to concentrate	Cracking knuckles
Decreased blood flow to skin	Unable to make decisions	Muscle twitching
Increased muscle tension (tightness)	Feeling confused	Pacing
Frequent urination	Feeling out of control	Scowling
Cramps/diarrhea, butterflies	Narrowing of attention	Yawning
Cotton mouth	Excitement	Shaking, trembling
Narrowing of visual field	Too charged, too pumped	Broken voice

AROUSAL, ANXIETY, AND PERFORMANCE

Mental preparation strategies such as goal setting, relaxation, imagery, positive self-talk, and mental preparation plans are employed to help an athlete gain or maintain control over excessive stress so that performance is possible at an optimal level of arousal. You must choose your most appropriate technique to moderate stress based on your knowledge of the skills to be performed (forward, defense, or goaltender) and based upon your personality and level of experience in hockey.

AROUSAL LEVEL AND PERFORMANCE

Performance effectiveness increases as arousal increases up to a certain zone. Beyond that point, further increases in arousal produce a decrease in performance. This theory has value for coaches who often believe their players are not sufficiently psyched or aroused. The body's natural response to excitement and fear is to secrete adrenaline which increases heart rate, blood pressure, respiratory rates, dilates the pupils, and can cause sweaty palms. Adrenaline is secreted in response to stimulation and the body cannot differentiate between excitement, which might be positive, and fears, which are negative.

AROUSAL LEVEL AND PERFORMANCE

Figure 3

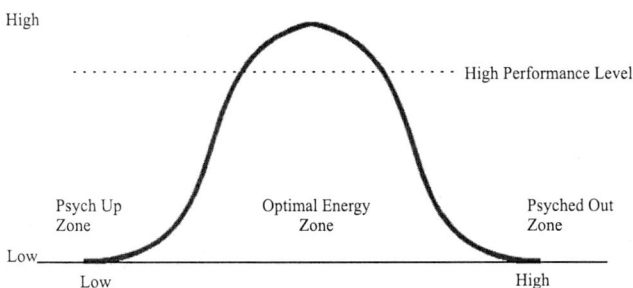

AROUSAL LEVEL

You must judge according to your position and your personality, the ideal level of arousal for you. Too little and you will have a flat, lackluster performance (will be in the psych-up zone) yet psyched too high (psyched out zone) and you may lose fluidity, pass too hard, and shoot too far; losing the soft hands, flexibility, and control you desire. I've known some players who are so psyched for each game that they are sick to their stomachs, irritable all day and yet they believe that at that high arousal level they will play their best. Others are calm, quietly focused, and yawning. All of these players may actually be at the best arousal level for themselves. By keeping a mental log book, it is easy to see when your best performances and practices occur. That information is then incorporated into your mental preparation plan.

CORRECTIONS

Players who are too flat need to intensify their psych-up strategies by setting higher, more challenging goals. Players who are too pumped up need to set less demanding goals combined with relaxation and calming imagery designed to reduce the tension they are experiencing (See Chapter 7). It is widely believed among sport psychologists that the 'Ideal Performance State' is a reflection of positive energy or arousal. This positively aroused state is characterized by an active mind and relaxed muscles which move on cue in a fluid, effortless manner. The negative state has the mind so activated that concentration is impaired, decisions can't be made, and muscles become tense and stiff.[22]

OPTIMAL FLOW ZONE

Figure 3 suggests that when a hockey player is performing in the *optimal flow zone* (The O-Zone), performance will be ideal. Too little or too much arousal and performance will suffer. Research I have done with my colleagues on hockey goalies reveals that there are wide variations in optimal energy zones (arousal levels) among individual goalies. All players must find their own ideal zones.

STANLEY CUP FINALS

Moments in sport like the Stanley Cup finals show that great effort produces great athletic achievements. Doug Jarvis wrote, "The circumstances surrounding those do or die games, when emotions are at their highest intensity, bring those games to a higher level. Jagr, Karyn Bye, Curtis Joseph, Cammy Granato, Matts Sundeen, Theoren Fleury, Michael Pecca, and Brett Hull are athletes who achieve and 'raise the bar' for others who will follow. And with the stage thus set, great players such as these invariably deliver virtuoso performances."[23] This phenomenon can best be

---

[22] Loehr, James *E. Mental Toughness Training for Sports.* (Penguin Books: New York, NY. 1982)   p. 57.
[23] Jarvis, Doug. *Hockey Magazine.*

understood by examining some of the tasks that need to be accomplished during a game or practice. While not all details of psychological and physiological responses to arousal will be discussed here, it is important to realize that arousal level might best be examined by looking at task-specific categories:

- Simple versus complex (a slap shot vs. a dipsy doodle)
- Small versus large muscle tasks (snap shot vs. a body check)
- Short term versus long term events (forwards tend to burst out each shift, whereas the goal tender is in for all three periods and sometimes overtime)

GENERAL GUIDELINES

A general guideline is that the simpler the task, the more large muscle motor units come into play. Optimum output for these types of tasks requires higher levels of arousal. For example, a weight lifter needs a short pure burst from many of the large muscle groups and the more pumped the lifter is, usually the better the chances for a successful lift. Conversely, more complex skills performed over a longer period of time require greater control of the small muscle groups in the body and best performance is achieved at a lower level of arousal. For instance, a golfer must have absolute control over the golf swing and cannot utilize high level energy bursts. Golfers must not become overly psyched or they will lose fine muscle control. Hockey requires a level of arousal somewhere between weight-lifting and golf. As mentioned earlier, it is critical you know what level of arousal works best for you. In sport psychology language, the *perceived challenge* rating must match the *perceived capability* if you are to be in the optimal flow zone. (See Diagram in Exercise 7)

MISSING THE OPTIMAL FLOW ZONE

It doesn't matter how a hockey player chooses to think of preparing to be in the optimal flow zone. Some might call it the ideal performance state, others may say that they have to find 'the flow', and still others think of it as getting 'psyched right'. These all refer to the psychic state during which mind and body are in balance and harmony. Thoughts must be positive, confident, and relaxed, yet energized. The more confidence you have in your ability to perform the necessary skills, the more likely you will be able to control your thinking to be in the o-zone.

You must realize, however, that it is very easy to miss the optimal level of arousal. By believing that an opposing team is not good and that your own team will dominate usually results in players falling short of their optimal arousal (missing the o-zone). In this situation, the player may come onto the ice flat, bored, and not psyched enough. On the other hand, if a player perceives the opposing team as consisting of vastly superior hockey players, it is easy to get psyched out. The player with this perspective of his opponents gets uptight and has no confidence. Consequently, it is the responsibility of each player to control his thinking to be in the o-zone.

STRATEGIES TO GET INTO THE OPTIMAL FLOW ZONE
(Figure 4)

When your team is playing a poorer team, it is important to remember that they have been practicing, they have a good coach, or that their goalie is capable of having a hot game. Think about your opponents coming out hustling and get yourself prepared accordingly. As a player, you might have to recall some of your own team's weaknesses such as starting your back-up goalie, having your two best players off with injuries, or that the game is on their home ice. These thoughts must be true in order to convince yourself of the need to get psyched up. Because of the equality among teams that exists in most leagues, it is usually easy to find the facts you might require to prepare appropriately for the challenge. This is what is meant when it is said of players like Theuren Fleury, Kevin Stevens, Shjon Podein, and Michael Pecca that they come ready to play each and every game. Once prepared for the game in this manner, the trick is to maintain it, shift-by-shift, period-by-period, game-by-game, and season-by-season.

The coach's task is to prepare the team as a unit. As a team, they must play confidently, be optimally aroused, and neither lack confidence nor be over cocky. A team, by definition, is made up of players. This means that every single player must be in their respective o-zones. By understanding the principles of arousal, players can learn what it feels like to find and sustain their own o-zones. Players can search their memories for feedback that will help identify the mental state compatible with their own best performance. The next two chapters will introduce Relaxation and Imagery, two of the skills which enhance the likelihood that a player will step on the ice in a mental state ready for peak performance. Relaxation and Imagery, along with Goal Setting, Mental Preparation Plans, and understanding how to get into the o-zone will provide you with a mental advantage.

Exercise 7

Finding Your Optimal Flow Zone

Instructions

1. Fill in the symptoms you want to feel to play in the o-zone for a good game, in spaces marked 1-5.

2. Mark for all five A's the thoughts you will need to get aroused and in the o-zone to play a team your team has defeated in the last three games.

3. Mark for all five B's a thought that you will need to get aroused and in the o-zone to play a team who has defeated your team twice, tied once, and who stands first in the league. Figure 4

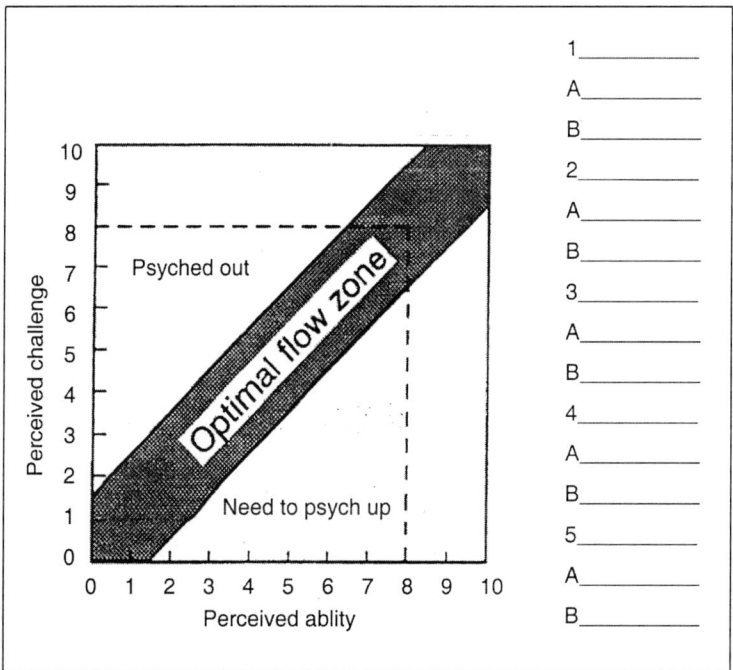

Form good habits. They are as hard to break as old ones.

Keep adapting this exercise as part of your pre-game preparation. It is a better way to occupy your mind than imagining unhealthy situations that might impede your success.

A winner is a person who asks questions and listens to the answer; A loser never listens.

AN ANECDOTE ON THE OPTIMAL FLOW ZONE

When my husband and I were assisting at a ski race, a little 8 year old downhill ski racer appeared in the starting gate. He had tight ski racing pants with a little stripe running down his leg. He wore a huge helmet and looked like a comma. The young skier was shivering from the cold. He huddled over the starting gate and awaited the count. We heard him mutter to himself, "Mind to Body, Are You Ready? ...Body to Mind, Let's Go!"

SELF-TEST 4: 2

1. Rate your knowledge of Arousal Level and the Optimal Flow Zone.

1	2	3	4	5
very low				*very high*

2. Rate your belief about the importance of Arousal Level and the Optimal Flow Zone.

1	2	3	4	5
very low				*very high*

3. Rate your planned use of Arousal Level and the Optimal Flow Zone.

1	2	3	4	5
very low				*very high*

Ask your mind and your body to learn from one another.

8

RELAXATION AND IMAGERY

**You must have a clear mental picture of the correct
thing before you can do it successfully
- Alex Morrison, Golf Teacher**

Brian Leetch has played hockey for Boston College,
the United States Olympic team, and currently plays for the
New York Rangers. After it was announced that he was a 'star'
in one of his first NHL games, he was interviewed and asked
if he felt pressure because he was playing a regular shift and
on the power play? His answer was, "Hey, that's my job, that's
not pressure, that's fun." Despite the pressures that surround
our lives, hockey can still be fun, even at the professional
level. Brian Leetch seems to have a relaxed yet committed
attitude. Other players like Chris Drury and Adam Deadmarsh
seem to have similar mental attitudes. Yet, not all players are
naturally so relaxed. Since mental skills are learned, players
who are willing to work can master relaxation skills that will
improve their mental toughness.

SELF-TEST 5: 1

1. Rate your knowledge of Relaxation Methods.

1	2	3	4	5
very low				*very high*

*2. Rate your belief about the importance of Relaxation
Methods.*

1	2	3	4	5
very low				*very high*

3. Rate your planned use of Relaxation Methods.

1	2	3	4	5
very low				very high

PURPOSES OF RELAXATION

Relaxation skills can give you a sense of control for both on and off ice situations. The specific purposes of relaxation are: (1) to lower heightened arousal and reduce undesired tension, (2) to create a pre-condition for learning imagery and mental rehearsal, (3) to serve as an exercise that promotes concentration, and (4) to provide a method for confronting specific fears.

RELAXATION TO CONTROL AROUSAL LEVEL AND REDUCE TENSION

A common complaint among athletes is the inability to relax prior to performance. Many hockey players experience muscle tenseness and claim that they 'feel tight'. This anxiety, and the corresponding muscular tightness, makes it difficult to do the skillful moves needed to perform well. Many hockey players prepare for games by listening to music and individualized relaxation tapes. Mentally tough hockey players know how much relaxation to use to produce the psych down effect that they desire or need.

ADAPTED RELAXATION METHOD

After reviewing several relaxation methods such as Benson's[24] and Jacobson's relaxation, autogenic training, yoga, and transcendental meditation, I have adapted a relaxation

---

[24] Benson, Herbert. *The Relaxation Response.* (William Morrow Co. Inc,.: New York, NY. 1976)

method[25] which is specifically suited to the athlete. It involves contracting and relaxing six muscle groups followed by a breathing period. During the breathing period, the focus is on moving air in and out of the lungs.[26] This relaxation method has been well received and found to be effective for most of the hockey players I have worked with. On the whole, the players seem to welcome the opportunity to learn strategies which can help them deal with pressure more effectively. When I am working with a team at a mental training meeting, we do this method as a group, otherwise it can be taught in individual sessions.

Hockey players instructed in relaxation are advised to use it in the afternoon or evening before a game as a prelude to imagery. It can also be used at any time they feel they are too tense to perform effectively. Hockey players are instructed to use this method before the National Anthem, before the opening face-off, on the bench, in the locker room, to wind down after a game, or to relax during travel. For example, when hockey players are standing for the anthem, they can pull their toes toward their chins, tighten their quads, pull in on the abdominals, clench fists within their gloves, tighten the biceps and triceps and lastly, pull up with the shoulders toward their ears. Each muscle group contraction is held for the count of 10. Deep breaths can then be taken, and players should be saying a word such as, 'calm, relax, peace, or slow' while releasing the air from the lungs. If time is short, each muscle group can simply be held in a contracted state for 5 seconds and the number of breaths limited. Practice the following method for simple muscle contractions and the corresponding breathing wherever and whenever you feel they may be beneficial.

---

[25] Smith, Scott, Wiese. (1990)
[26] Benson, Ibid.

Exercise 8

ADAPTED RELAXATION METHOD INSTRUCTIONS

Suggestions

1. Practice in a quiet, comfortably warm room where there are minimal distractions.

2. Attention must be focused on your own breathing.

3. It is essential to have a passive attitude and to let thoughts and images move through your mind easily. If your thoughts begin to wander, gently bring them back to focus.

4. While you should be comfortable, it is important not to get so comfortable that sleep occurs.

Instructions

1. Sit in a comfortable position (eyes open or closed).

2. Start by pulling your toes up toward your nose while contracting your calf muscles as hard as possible for a count of 10. Release. Relax.

3. Become aware of the relaxation that follows.

4. Repeat this process while tightening your quadriceps. Hold for 10. Release. Relax. Become aware of the relaxation that follows.

5. Now Tighten your abdominals as hard as you can. Hold for 10. Release. Relax. Become aware of the relaxation

that follows.

6. Tighten your biceps. Hold for 10. Release. Relax. Become aware of the relaxation that follows.

7. Pull your shoulders toward your ears. Hold for 10. Release. Relax. Become aware of the relaxation that follows.

8. Now that your muscles are relaxed, begin with deep breathing. Each inhalation and exhalation should be slow and full. When exhaling, you may want to repeat the word "calm" or something that reminds you of the purpose of your relaxation exercise.

9. Allow all the air to escape your lungs, like a deflated balloon, before beginning the next breath.

10. Continue the breathing exercise for at least 10 minutes concentrating on nothing but the movement of the air in and out of your lungs.

RELAXATION AS AN EXERCISE IN CONCENTRATION

If relaxation is used as an exercise in concentration, the emphasis is on breathing, with your concentration on the movement of air in and out of your lungs. The period of concentration should last about as long as the 'shift or skill' requires concentration and the absence of distracting thoughts. A forward or defenseman needs the length of a shift while the goaltender needs to concentrate for an entire period of play. Total absorption for the length of time you wish to train for is the objective of this exercise.

As you practice this technique, you will become effective in reducing tension which, in turn, leads to an increase in your sense of control. Relaxation skills provide players with an effective buffer against an overly zealous coach or parents who, although well intentioned, may frighten or over excite the players. Relaxation skills can also be used to decrease the effect of 'hype' created by the media. Generally, relaxation skills are helpful to control anxiety before public speaking engagements, try-outs, or off-ice situations in life where stress and pressure are experienced. They are helpful in the 'Beyond Hockey Period'.

RELAXATION TO CONFRONT SPECIFIC FEARS

It is impossible to think simultaneously of two emotions that require opposite physiological responses. For example, it is impossible to be both relaxed and in a state of fear at the same time. Therefore, an athlete who is struggling with a particular fear can be de-sensitized if the feared event is thought of during a period of relaxation. Imagine, for example, that a player has a phobia of skating in on a breakaway and shooting wide of the net. The hockey player might fear the embarrassment of choking when the chance was there to come through for the team. When asked to imagine the scene in the mind's eye while in the relaxed state, the player is able to see the shot miss the net but will be unable to feel the symptoms of tension and shame. Consequently, the anxiety provoking image readily loses its power to upset the player as the association between the fear of choking is separated from the uncomfortable feelings associated with the imagined failure. Gradually, as the feared event loses its power to generate anxiety, it moves from being a major phobia to an event that causes only mild concern. Imagery can then be used to change the image of failure into an image of success. Regardless of the reason relaxation is used, the method described in this chapter will be suitable for most hockey players.

SELF-TEST 5:2

1. Rate your knowledge of Relaxation Methods.

1	2	3	4	5
very low				*very high*

2. Rate your belief about the importance of Relaxation Methods.

1	2	3	4	5
very low				*very high*

3. Rate your planned use of Relaxation Methods.

1	2	3	4	5
very low				*very high*

9

MENTAL IMAGERY

Picture yourself vividly as winning and that alone will contribute immeasurably to your success

I really believe if you visualize yourself doing something, you can make that image come true
–Wayne Gretzky

SELF-TEST 6:1

1. Rate your knowledge of Mental Imagerv.

1	2	3	4	5
very low				very high

2. Rate your belief about the importance of Mental Imagery.

1	2	3	4	5
very low				very high

3. Rate your planned use of Mental Imagery.

1	2	3	4	5
very low				very high

During the 1986 season, the baseball pitcher Corbett made four consecutive appearances for the California Angels where he earned four saves and held the opposition scoreless for 12 1/2 innings. He gave credit to sport psychologist, Ken Ravizza, who had worked with the Angels' pitching staff. Corbett had spent time on the disabled list during the past three seasons and said, "In the past, I pitched five minutes on the side every day to stay sharp. Now, I can do that pitching in my mind and save the wear and tear on my arm."[27] Many players in all sports have developed their imagery skills to the point that it has become a big factor in their athletic success. Mark McGwire uses mental imagery as do many professionals in medicine and other fields.

RELAXATION AS A PRECONDITION TO IMAGERY

Research shows that imagery is more effective when combined with relaxation. When hockey players are relaxed, and their concentration is focused on their breathing, their minds become free of distractions and the images they select are vivid, clearer, and more helpful. Imagery is the vivid recollection or idealization of a specific skill or event. Most images are created by the individual or are drawn from memory. But images can also be a reconstruction of a previous event or any mental patterns or pictures that help the athlete focus upon key performances and effectiveness. It is more than just visualizing (seeing an experience in the mind's eye) as it should involve touch, sound, sight, feeling, and smell. It includes the kinesthetic sense which is the sensation of body position and the presence or absence of movement. This sensation arises from nerve endings in muscles, tendons, and joints. This is a highly developed sense in most hockey players for whom balance, quickness, agility, and an awareness of where the body is in space are essential to performance.

As you begin to master imaging yourself performing on the ice, you should also experience the appropriate emotional mood state which accompanies these events. That is, you should not just see yourself in a detached way, but rather begin to encounter the events and performances as if

---

[27] Dorfman, H.A. and Karl Kuehl. *The Mental Game of Baseball: A Guide to Peak Performance.* (Diamond communications: Southbend, IN. 1991) p. 139.

they really happened, including the attending emotions. Joy, excitement, dejection, determination, tension, anger, and pain are examples of emotions that may be linked to your on-ice experiences.

PURPOSES OF IMAGERY IN ICE HOCKEY

The purposes of using imagery in ice hockey are to assist in the learning and mental practice of complex motor skills. Specifically, this means:

1. Mentally practicing individual hockey skills such as stick handling, skating drills, checking, goal tending, shooting, and passing.

2. Mentally practicing skills that involve opponents or linemates, such as face-offs, break-out plays, 3 on 2's, 2 on 1's, etc.

3. Mentally practicing hockey situations such as the power play, a man short, or specific chalk talk situations that have been taught by the coach.

4. As you prepare for a game, it is important to mentally anticipate and picture yourself in the setting. This means imaging the arena, the locker room, the interactions with teammates, coach, opponents, referees, and preparing for the influence of the crowd.

5. Imagine the 'self-discipline' you will need to avoid situations in which you would otherwise take numerous penalties. See yourself behaving in a controlled, disciplined manner.

Some players use a pre-performance video to help imagine the performance they want to have. For example, Ron Hextall, who just retired from goaltending in the NHL (1999), had a pre-performance video of outstanding saves spliced together and taped to the music *In The Heat of The Night* by Bryan Adams. Hextall reportedly used his pre-performance videotape before the Canada Cup. This method of imaging has a sound basis in modeling theory. Coaches also frequently use these methods. Glen Sather, who coached the Edmonton Oilers to several Stanley Cup victories frequently used a video of the Oilers defeating the Montreal Canadians. Sather played this videotape of the victory with Tom Jones singing 'The Impossible Dream' in the locker room just before a final Stanley Cup game.

SUPPORT FOR IMAGERY

In sport, athletes such as Jack Nicklaus, Greg Louganis, Nancy Kerrigan, and Wayne Gretzky have all claimed imagery to be a powerful enhancer of specific sport skills. [28] Mark McGwire routinely practices mental preparation, which I believe includes imagery.

The most convincing support for the use of imagery has been found through many scientific studies. Research shows that basketball players who used imagery improved 15% more than those who simply practiced shooting but did not use imagery. A study that examined basketball free throws showed that a group who practiced relaxation and imagery together improved significantly over a group who used relaxation or imagery alone. Furthermore, a study on NHL hockey players found that imaging successful off-ice outcomes not related to hockey resulted in an improvement of on-ice performances. Hockey players who imaged life

---

[28] Martens, Ranier. *Coaches Guide to Sport Psychology.* (Human Kinetics: Champaign, IL. 1987)

expectancy situations positively (optimists) had more points gained from goals and assists than those who viewed the same off-ice situations negatively (pessimists).[29]

EXPERIENCE IN JUNIOR HOCKEY

Over the past four years, the Junior team I have worked with has imaged specific skills; home games, away games, penalty provoking situations, and the national championship games. Imagery sessions are always started with relaxation routines. The team members were asked to mentally splice their own pre-performance videos against background music in their heads as a part of their mental preparation. At the national, junior national, and professional levels it is worthwhile to ensure that all interested players have individualized audio cassettes to play as they prepare for competition. As players become increasingly proficient at imagery skills, they practice more difficult skills, seeing themselves successfully completing greater and greater on-ice challenges.

PREPARING FOR MENTAL IMAGERY

The vividness and control of an image is found to be best when:
1. You are in a setting which has few distractions.
2. You are relaxed yet attentive.

* Relaxation is important to reduce brain activity such as analyzing past mistakes, worrying about exams, hockey performance, or a girlfriend. Such concerns will interfere with your ability to effectively image the desired performance.

Relaxed attention releases imagery; tension suppresses it

[29] Davis, Hap. *Perceptual and Motor Skills*

3. You have the self-motivation to train. A commitment is necessary to practice imagery regularly. Just like physical practice, mental imagery improves with repetition.

4. You must have the right attitude and proper level of expectations. Imagery is more successful when you expect it to help. The images produced are more vivid and stable when you really believe in them

Negativism and self-doubt neutralize images just as they diminish athletic performances

5. Systematic practice is necessary. As with practicing physical skills in ice hockey, it is not the quantity but the quality of mental practice that is important. It is important to identify what you wish to accomplish and then set up specific images of the hockey skills or situations that need mental practice.

6. Resist the temptation to practice skills you are already good at and instead select weaknesses or poorly understood plays and subject them to vivid, controlled, and systematic imagery sessions.

IMAGERY TIPS

Frequently imagery is first taught at a very basic level. Athletes might be asked to focus on specific objects[30] or on 3 colored baseballs, placed in various positions in the mind's eye.[31] Readers are referred to these guides that describe these

---

[30] Harris, Dorothy and Bette Harris. *The Athlete's Guide to Sports Psychology: Mental Skills For Physical People.* (Leisure Press: New York, NY 1984.) p. 110.

[31] Dorfman, H.A. and Karl Kuehl. *The Mental Game of Baseball: A*

methods if they wish additional information.

In summary:

1. You should master your relaxation skills before trying to learn imagery.

2. Once in a relaxed state, you can picture yourself in your home uniform, away uniform, from within, from beside yourself and standing facing the flag, before the start of a game, etc.

3. While seeing yourself standing in your skates, you should next feel your stick in your gloves, the pressure of your laced skates and your helmet in your hand. Are your hands sweaty'? Is your heart pounding and your mouth dry? Can you feel the emotions of excitement or fear'? Can you hear the anthem, or hear the sticks bang on the ice, or hear coughs or calls from the crowd? Proper imaging can bring all these physical and mental sensations into greater focus so that you can really be in the game.

4. When you are 'all there', on the ice, it is the right time to start mentally practicing the skills you will be expected to perform.

*This is not a daydreaming session, but rather a planned, disciplined period with specific skills and plays you want to successfully image.

In conclusion, imagery is an excellent mental strategy to practice the hockey skills for which you already have a 'blueprint' in place. It is also an excellent way to stay sharp

Guide to Peak Performance. (Diamond communications: Southbend, IN. 1991) p. 148.

during rehabilitation from an injury as it allows for mental practice without subjecting the athlete to the risk of another injury. Imagery can be helpful in identifying errors, making corrections, and practicing the corrected image until the skill *is* being executed perfectly.

Be Bold and Mighty Forces Will Come to Your Aid – Basil King, Conquest of Fear

Exercise 9

The Pendulum[32]

Imagined events should produce responses similar to those of an actual experience. Images from the brain transmit impulses to the muscles for execution of the imagined skill, even though these impulses may be minor and produce movement that is almost undetectable. To illustrate that movement occurs as a result of vivid imagery, try this simple experiment.

(a) Make a pendulum from a 10" piece of string and tie a bolt or a ring shaped item on it.

(b) Draw a circle and divide it into four quarters.

(c) Do your Relaxation technique.

(d) Hold the string between the thumb and forefinger. The pendulum will move on its own at first but soon it will swing in whatever direction you will want it to swing. Close your eyes and try it.

---

[32] Martens, Ranier. *Coaches Guide to Sport Psychology.* (Human Kinetics: Champaign, IL. 1987)

(e) Concentrate on visualizing the pendulum swinging in a specific direction. Intently imagine the motion, thinking about nothing else. Avoid intentionally moving your hands.

(f) Open your eyes and see if the experiment was successful.

(g) Reverse the order. Think about the shapes on the diagram.

To demonstrate that the slight firings of neural pathways occur as a result of imagery, Dr. Richard Suinn placed electrodes on the leg muscles of a downhill ski racer. Using EMT (electromyography), Suinn obtained electrical patterns in the muscles of the skier during an imagery session that closely paralleled the electrical patterns of the skier's muscles that would be expected had he actually been skiing.[33]

Exercise 10

An excellent offensive exercise for forwards and defense is to look at a photo of a goal net with the goalie in position and to have the players see only the open parts of the net. Gretzky stated in his book that the best goal scorer's never know the details of the opponent's goal tender. What they look for when coming in on goal, is open net, whereas, poor goal score's can tell you the brand of the goalies' pads, gloves, etc. Obviously, poor goal score's fix their eyes on where the goalie is, instead of where he's not. You want to see the empty space, the open area of the net. If scoring goals is important to you, then it is essential that your eye be attracted to the open area of netting. Imagine it covered with brightly colored lights or red ribbons

[33] Suinn, Richard. *Visual Motor Behavioral Rehearsal* p.67.

to attract your eye away from the goalie.

IN THIS EXERCISE

Hockey players are asked to imagine how many pucks they could put in the open area above, through the 5-hole, or to the right or left of the goalie. Because the puck is so small (weighs only 3 oz), players can usually see 30-40 good shots. Players are then asked to draw the pucks in the net with a line to show where the puck was shot from. The exercise can be extended to include a percentage of rebound shots for second and third efforts.

This photo shows Shjon Podein, in front of the net (no goalie in pads available that day) with 24 pucks piled on top of each other, and I believe, it was 26 pucks across, end to end. Since the 24 in the column to his right occupy less than half the vertical, readers will accept the notion that 48 pucks can be piled up inside a net. If we use the formula for the area of a rectangle 2(L) x 2(W) = 2 (24) x 2(28) = 48 x 96 = approximately 4,608 pucks can fit inside the open net at any one time. If we are generous and allow that a goalie can protect 2/3 of the net, there is still space for 1,536 pucks! Think about that! (Concept courtesy of Tom Pederson - San Jose Sharks).

SELF-TEST 6:2

1. Rate Your knowledge of Mental Imagery.

1	*2*	*3*	*4*	*5*
very low				*very high*

2. Rate your belief about the importance of Mental Imagery.

1	*2*	*3*	*4*	*5*
very low				*very high*

3. Rate your planned use of Mental Imagery.

1	*2*	*3*	*4*	*5*
very low				*very high*

10

CONCENTRATION AND CONFIDENCE

Winners Believe They Can Win

Concentration is fundamental to playing the game of hockey, yet it is rarely explained or discussed. Suggestions on how to improve concentration are almost never made to hockey players even though proper concentration is an essential ingredient of successful performance.

A sport psychologist once shared a good anecdote about concentration in sport.[34] The story was about a little boy playing goalie in his first soccer game. The little boy's shoe came untied late in the game and he didn't know how to tie it. He left the goal and looked for his mother who was sitting in the 5th row of the bleachers. Embarrassed that a goal might be scored while the family's hope for the future was having his shoe tied, she hustled him back to his job in goal. The whole team swarmed after the ball (bee-hive soccer) which never came near his end. He sat down and started trying to tie his shoe. After 6 or 7 minutes he got it! At just about the same time, the referee's whistle blew to signal the end of the game. His little team rushed down, picked him up, and carried him off the field. Proudly, he pointed his foot out for all to see, certain that the celebration was because he had learned to tie his shoes. He had no idea that he had earned a shutout and that his team had won.

One of my daughters was jumping a horse in a medal round. When she came down a line of jumps she failed to see the correct distance and failed to lengthen her horse's stride. Consequently, the horse took off from too far back,

---

[34] Lewallen, Jack Dr. Sport psychology presentation in Minneapolis, 1986.

landing on a huge spread jump. He flipped over and landed on his side, pinning her underneath. Later when I asked her what happened, she said that she lost her concentration and at the time of the accident she had been thinking about going shopping! A lack of concentration toward the task at hand can lead to some scary results.

One well known coach, Ken Johannson, talks about situations in youth hockey. He described how misleading it was, as a coach, to think that your players would know exactly what to do just because you reviewed a play with them in a chalk talk; right wing will pass to center who will pass to left wing and so on. But what the coach doesn't know is that the little boy skating down on the right wing with the puck is thinking, "If I can get this puck in the net and score, my Grandma in the stands will take me to the Dairy Queen after the game."

However, lack of concentration isn't limited to youngsters. Many high school, junior, college, and professional hockey players also have difficulty maintaining their concentration throughout a long game. One player, now in Division I, confided that he was so embarrassed about how he looked on the ice in his poorly fitting uniform that he'd pass the puck anywhere just to get rid of it and take the attention away from himself. If this is what he was thinking about, he was not concentrating on the game he was playing.

IMPROVING CONCENTRATION IN HOCKEY

Part of the purpose of mental preparation plans is to encourage players to attend to the details necessary for getting totally into the game, mentally and physically. Ensuring in advance that uniforms fit properly and preparing for other distractions helps prevent loss of concentration. Structuring for the ideal conditions while anticipating and being prepared tor adverse conditions greatly reduces the likelihood of a loss in concentration.

Hockey players should be trained to concentrate and stay tuned in to the mind-body connection for the length of time the player typically needs to perform without a break. Forwards and defense need to practice concentrating for the length of their shift then allow a few seconds of free association before refocusing for the next shift. The goal tender has varying degrees of intensity of focus. Generally, he must have his head in the game for the entire period, although concentration is more intense when the puck is being repeatedly shot on his own goal compared to when it is at the other end.

RELAXATION ENHANCES CONCENTRATION

The best exercise to enhance concentration is to try maintaining focus for the specific period of time you are on the ice during practice and in games. As you become successful at concentrating on each shift, you must reward yourself, take a break, and then refocus. Concentration requirements are sport-specific. There is no reason for a hockey player to stay focused for 2 and 1/2 hours, the length of a good marathon while it is equally useless for a runner to learn to concentrate only for the length of a hockey shift. When lapses in concentration occur in hockey, they must be brief, and if they are to occur at all, they must not occur on the ice. On the bench or in the locker room is a better place than on the ice but if they do occur on the ice, you must rapidly detect the lapses and refocus quickly.

In addition to on-ice concentration exercises, the focus on breathing which occurs during relaxation should be practiced for the same length of time as a hockey shift (30-50 seconds). A focus on the flow of air moving in and out of you lungs, once mastered, can easily be substituted with a focus on the flow state of a hockey shift. Each skill that is to be imaged can be imaged for the length of a shift as well. This promotes concentration for appropriate periods of play. The objective is to gradually extend the length and quality of your concentration. Practice concentrating for overtime periods as well, mindful that the NCAA Championship in 1991 went into 3 overtime periods. Specifically, if the average player skates 30-45 second shifts, 6-8 shifts per period, three periods per game, players would need to expect approximately 21-22 minutes of ice time in a regulation game. A 30 minute imagery practice session could allow for 20 (1 minute) imaging 'flow' spots with 30 second breaks in between. A session of that length would ensure that most face-offs, breakaways, pass patterns, scoring opportunities, and two-way transitional play, etc. can be mentally rehearsed. Similar sessions prior to practice will enhance the quality of the on-ice practice session.

CONCENTRATION PATTERNS FOR HOCKEY PLAYERS

FORWARDS AND DEFENSE

1. You should take a deep breath to focus just as you step over the boards to re-enter a game.

2. Cue statements such as 'I'm all there, focused, and in the play' are helpful when combined with words such as 'intensity', 'aggressiveness', and 'patience'. Anything which helps you focus on optimal performance may be used.

3. As skaters leave the ice, their minds often wander for a few seconds while they breathe deeply to replenish oxygen. This is normal and is to be expected. However, you must soon evaluate your effectiveness

and identify strategies for the next shift. This may include attempting to lower shots, tying up the center on the face-off, communicating with linemates, or 'clicking' off anger responses and other negative thoughts.

4.   Then, you should watch intently while getting your head back into the flow, the pace, and the details of the game. As your turn comes to go back on the ice, the sequence is repeated: deep breath, cue words, focus, etc.

GOALIES

Among hockey players there tends to be a preoccupation with the 'goalie mystique'. This makes players fearful of rocking the boat when a goaltender is on a hot streak or can prompt them to leave the goaltender alone to 'slumpbust' when he's not. Goaltenders must not be denied the same opportunity to learn mental skills that are available to other players. If the team is afraid of breaking a goaltender's hot streak then the team is sending the message to the goalie that his performance is externally controlled. That insinuates that the goalie is influenced more by luck than by the ability and effort he puts into his performance.

SPECIFICS FOR GOALTENDERS

Although goaltenders should be included in the exercises listed above, they do occupy a unique position on the ice and encounter different concentration challenges. The following is a short list of tips specific to goaltenders:

1.   Goaltenders need to concentrate for longer periods than do forwards and defensemen.

2. One of the problems that goaltenders face as they move up the ranks from high school to juniors, to college, and finally to the NHL, is staying associated and concentrating for these longer time periods. Because the number of shots they have to face on net increases dramatically, as does the speed of the releases, the speed of turnovers, and the specd of breakaways, the goalies are forced to keep their heads in the game for longer periods. In the 1991 NCAA championship game, it took Northern Michigan 3 overtimes to beat Boston College. Imagine the concentration required for both goaltenders that night (ending at 2 am). The Minnesota State High School championship was won after five overtime periods and the 1999 Stanley Cup was won by the Dallas Stars (on a questionable goal) in the 3rd overtime period.

3. Practice sessions for goaltenders using relaxation and focusing on their breathing must be extended to the length of a period. These periods of concentration can be broken up by whistles, etc. The closer concentration drills are to simulating actual game conditions, the more helpful they will be. Therefore concentration drills such as relaxation and imagery should train the goalie to focus on making save after save with all senses involved for the length of time that game conditions might require.

4. Goalies must make use of the few pauses that line changes, penalties and face-offs might allow. During this time, the goalie has a short physical and mental break. This is the time to stand up straight, stretch, let the mind wander briefly, and then regain concentration.

5. Many goaltenders I know actively keep their concentration by staying physically or verbally involved in the game. Even if there is not much action at their end, some have rituals of banging the goal pipes, talking to the referees, teammates, or opponents. There are any number of activities to help them stay engaged in the game. These interactions help some goalies remain alert and reactive. Other goalies stay totally focused (i.e., Ed Belfour of the Dallas Stars during the 1999 Stanley Cup appeared calm and self-contained as opposed to the Buffalo Sabres goalie, Dominique Hasek, who was very integrated into all aspects of the game.) Find what works best for you and use it.

Professional goaltenders are also concerned with effectively maintaining concentration. Ken Dryden used to make a ritual of the whole day of a game. This extended right through to his dressing routine. He dressed at a steady, preoccupying pace: at 7:07, he donned his pants, by 7:12 skates, by 7:17 pads, by 7:20 vest and sweater. Dryden had this to say about his ritual and mental preparation, "Too fast and with nothing to do, I think about the game or whatever else comes into my mind, too slow, and I rush and by rushing I wonder if I've somehow affected *how I will* play. Not wanting to think about the game or something other than the game, I keep rigidly on a schedule. I want to arrive at game time, undistracted, my mind blank, my emotions under control. If I can do that, the rest of me is ready."[35] Ken Dryden's ritualized dressing routine promoted a positive, firm concentration which was absorbing enough to prevent negative thoughts from entering his mind.

---

[35] Dryden, Ken. *The Game*. (Penguin Books: New York, NY. 1983) p. 171.

Ron Hextall, the goaltender who has scored goals, speaks of his first game in the NHL when he started for Philadelphia against the Edmonton Oilers, "I didn't pay much attention to the crowd or fans because I was concentrating so much on the game. I was extremely nervous. Who wouldn't be, and when I saw Gretzky skating around, I simply told myself, 'Just play hard, that's all that you can do'".

CHANNEL CLICKING' AND CONCENTRATION
(Exercise 11)

One strategy to enhance concentration is called 'channel clicking'. It is a basic exercise in *negative thought-stopping*. The more technical name for it *is cognitive restructuring. I* believe the person who introduced me to this concept was Dr. Wayne Halliwell, who demonstrated 'channel clicking' at a meeting over a decade ago in Montreal. One has to imagine that the mind is a television set with 3 channels; the positive, negative, and escape channel. Thoughts that cross a player's mind must be identified as belonging to one of these three channels. If the thought is labeled 'positive' and is a thought that contributes to confidence and performance, it is allowed to remain on the screen. If a thought is evaluated as negative, it is 'clicked off and replaced with a thought from the positive channel. A positive thought such as, 'Yes, you'll stay onside, you can do it, hustle' is offered in place of the negative thought.

The escape channel can be programmed with positive images, thoughts, cue words, and quotes that enhance the athlete's performance. (Many of the quotes taken from Sports-Minded provided in this book could be memorized and put on the escape channel). When a positive thought is not immediately available to counter a negative thought, a quick switch to the escape channel might permit a peek at the image of your team winning Nationals, the sensation of joy you'll feel, or an image of how a hero like Brett Hull, Steve Yzerman, Mike Pecca, Patrick Roy, or Cammy Granato might react in the same situation. Players fill their own escape channels with images or memories that inspire them to perform at their best.

Channel Clicking is an excellent strategy for keeping tabs on concentration. When you are in the o-zone, your mind and body are totally in the game and you won't need this technique. But if you are aware something is wrong, you can train yourself to scan your thoughts, identify which thoughts you are having, and channel click appropriately to get mentally back into the game.

Cynthia Cooper, who plays for the Houston Comets in the WNBA, has on three occasions been awarded the MVP of the WNBA trophy. Her coach speaks highly of her, paying her the ultimate compliment awarded an athlete in any sport, "She is the most focused basketball player I have ever seen".

I guess more players lick themselves than are ever licked by an opposing team. The first thing any man has to know is how to handle himself – Connie Mack

SPORTS CONFIDENCE

Research indicates that a belief in personal competence will positively influence performance, assuming that an individual has the necessary physical skills. Confidence can influence arousal level, concentration, decision making, expended effort, and the persistence required to overcome certain difficulties. It is said of Chris Chelios, the first American born player to win the Norris Trophy for best defenseman, "Chris wants to play as a winner and will do everything in his power to achieve that end, he loves the game." Chris Drury has the same look and I believe his coaches speak of him in a similar manner. I'm also certain that Ben Smith would say the same thing about Karyn Bye.

Sport confidence can be viewed on a continuum from diffidence (too little confidence) to over-confidence (too much confidence). Optimal or ideal levels of sport confidence fall between these 2 extremes.[36] The figure below illustrates this

Figure 5

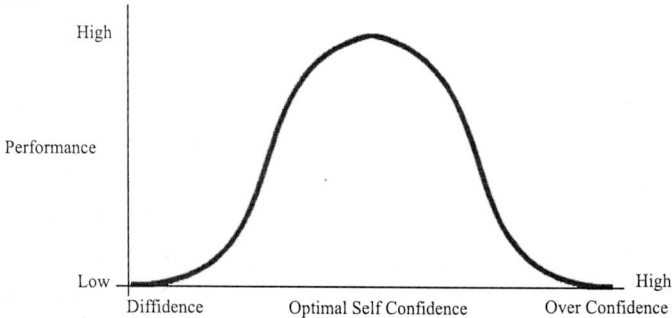

continuum.

Confidence is the basic belief or trust which one has in oneself. Thus, 'sport confidence' pertains to an athlete's confidence in his or her ability to achieve in a given sport. Sport confidence is not what the athlete hopes to do in sport but what a player realistically expects to do. Hockey players may develop on-ice confidence but lack confidence off-ice in social or academic situations. Sport confidence also varies within a sport, fluctuating with one's perceived mastery of specific skills. For example, in hockey, a goaltender may be confident in his or her ability to stop all shots except those that are high on his or her stick side. A forward may have confidence in most situations except in the face-off circle or on the power play. A defenseman may excel in all aspects of his or her game yet may choke on 2-on-1 situations. Identifying where confidence is lacking will reveal which skills need physical and mental practice.

[36] Martens, Ranier. *Coaches Guide to Sport Psychology*. (Human Kinetics: Champaign IL. 1987)

OPTIMAL SELF-CONFIDENCE

Athletes with optimal self-confidence set realistic goals based on their own ability (Chapter 4). Self-confident athletes play within themselves, developing their competence and confidence simultaneously. There is a direct relationship between competence levels and confidence. As competence in a skill improves, the sport confidence grows. And as confidence increases, a player is likely to try new things and strengthen weaker skills. This increases overall competence. But all the confidence in the world will not replace having the physical skills and knowledge essential for the particular sport. That is why players must have a realistic self-perception about their potential and physical ability. However, the converse is also true; developing physical skills in the absence of self confidence results in poor performance. Competence and confidence must be developed and nurtured together because having one without the other will not be conducive to optimal performance.

GAINING SELF-CONFIDENCE[37] (Dr. Merry Miller)

1. It has been said that 'Nothing breeds success like success'. Early success enhances an athlete's motivation to persist in an activity. Coaches should structure practices to ensure that all team members engage in confidence-building activities. When children begin hockey, practicing without a goalie enhances confidence as does a careful increase in the challenges provided. Too often athletes are moved up too quickly. At each higher level, more time is needed to adjust to the size, speed, and skill of the game. Successes at each level should be internalized

---

[37] Miller, Merry . *Sport Confidence.* Sports Psychology Training Bulletin.

(accepted by the athlete) before the hockey player climbs to the next rung on the ladder. That is why formative years in junior and college hockey are extremely important to players moving up to the NHL.

2. Athletes must be given permission to fail. If hockey players know they won't be ridiculed for mistakes, they can invest their total energies into achieving success rather than expending their energy avoiding failures.

3. Hockey players will benefit most by learning from positive role models, particularly when the model is a skilled player of nearly the same age or a little older. Ideally, a youngster should feel 'If he can do it, I will, too'. If, however, the role model is too far ahead of the player who is trying to copy the performance, the response might be, 'Well, he should be able to do that, he is a pro and I'm just a pee-wee'.

4. Role modeling is a positive facilitator of success as long as the skills are well displayed and the observer can identify with the role-model.

5. Use positive self-statements. These self-statements are constructed to reinforce the positive behavior you want to accomplish. For example, 'I am cool, relaxed, I am focused', should replace 'I will not choke.' The mind does not have a mental picture or image for 'I will not', so it reacts only to the word 'choke'. All statements that are intended to be positive and self-affirming must be stated in positive, rather than negative ways!

6. Own your successes. It is important to attribute

successes to internal factors such as consistent hard work, intense concentration, and good preparation. It is important to reflect on your successes, internalize them and make them a part of you.

As Dr. Terry Orlick has said, "The best performance you have ever had should become who you are as a hockey player. For if, that best performance was within you to come out once, it can appear time and time again if you allow it to happen." Often hockey players think of a peak performance as something that just happened when 'I was playing that game at an exceptionally high level'. They might regard it as a freak occurrence, something they don't own and one that is not likely to happen again. This is not true, keep it, it's yours.

The mental preparation plans suggested in Chapter 5 are based on the belief that the best players recapture those peak experiences and learn how to put them back to back, one after the other. Their method is confidence and consistency.

BUILDING AND MAINTAINING CONFIDENCE THROUGH IMAGERY

Hockey players can use the imagery techniques described in Chapter 9 to see themselves practicing the desired performance which builds and maintains confidence. For example, centers should see themselves getting face-offs at crucial times in big games. Practice success, then practice coping with adversity, then prepare for competition by imaging success in competition again.

If a player is having difficulty imagining success in a certain skill, it is helpful to watch a role model (Watch Jaromir Jagr, Peter Forsberg, or Mike Pecca move in on goal, Curtis Joseph make a save, or Kevin Stevens on defense). Then do relaxation and imagery to see the role model doing it in your mind's eye. Then imagine yourself doing it and add the other emotions which most closely approximate the real thing. You can do all this in your mind! Then on the ice, make "it" happen just as you mentally practiced.

In conclusion, sport confidence in ice hockey is a player's belief in his ability to execute the skills necessary to produce a particular performance outcome. A player can intensify his belief in his ability to execute hockey skills by working on the exercises outlined in this chapter. A good player is one who really believes in himself.

"The Flower skated wide along the boards and wound up for a sharp-angle slapshot from 40 feet away. It was a classic Lafleur bomb, beating the Bruins' goalie to the long side. Lafleur and only Lafleur could have scored on that long shot! It couldn't have been a more perfect shot, our spirits just soared." According to Doug Jarvis, who at the time also played for Montreal, "Moments like that are made for that type of player. You know they are the ones who are going to do it for you"! Brett Hull and Mike Modano knew much was expected of them in the 1999 Stanley Cup finals. They clearly established themselves as "franchise" players.

Invest your total energy into achieving success and not in avoiding failure

Exercise 11

CHANNEL CLICKING

The players are asked to sit in a circle, each holding a clicker-type ball point pen which serves as their remote controller. From the standpoint of an exercise, all players, one at a time, contribute a thought that frequently crosses their minds before or during a competition. The rest of the team listens and evaluates whether the thought is positive or negative. If it is positive, the next player takes his turn. If a negative thought is expressed, the team all click their pens. The player then has to come up with a restructuring, positive thought. If he cannot come up with a thought that is satisfactory, the team helps out. For example, 'I'm offside again, the coach is going to bench me' would be interpreted as negative. While it may be true, it offers nothing constructive to help avoid being offside again. The team would click it off. A countering thought would be 'I'll communicate with my center, so we avoid this. I'll keep my eye on the puck carrier, and if he's not going to pass, I'll quickly cut to get parallel to the blue line'.

When it is necessary to go to the escape channel, the player might draw a deep breath according to his relaxation skills and affirm his own value with, 'You are good', or some equally affirmative statement. Self-affirming statements can be stored on the escape channel as can quotations and images of heroes that are inspiring. The escape channel should be thought of as the place where mental skills and positive self-statements are stored during the game and used later for reference. Positive quotations and thoughts prevent a player from becoming negative and berating himself.

TEAM DISCUSSION GUIDELINES AFTER CHANNEL CLICKING EXERCISE

(a) How did the game provide insight into positive and negative statements unique to each player's position (allows players to get better acquainted)'?

(b) How did the channel clicking game heighten an athlete's awareness of self-talk when it is negative and counterproductive to a good performance'?

(c) How did the activity of clicking become symbolic of a mental correction easily used during a game or between periods'?

(d) How can an escape channel be programmed to have positive self-talk, quotes, images, and motivational thoughts that can be put into play when needed'?

Channel clicking is a positive strategy to assist the hockey player with a method of quickly changing thinking modes. Adversity, anger, and other negative situations can be detected and countered until the player is off the ice and can deal with the situation effectively. The mark of top players is the ability to quickly rally and regain poise after a negative or devastating event. Shjon Podein told me about an incidence that occurred when he was playing for the USA in the World Hockey Tournament. He came back to the bench frustrated and acting out, slamming his stick around. Walt Kyle, the coach, said, "Come on Shjon, click that off; what if Aynsley were here!" Shjon said he chuckled because it came out of the blue and surprised him, but he realized he was letting his emotions get out of control. He clicked, settled down, and re-gained his focus.

Exercise 12

Dr. Miller suggests the creation of a Sports Confidence Bank in which personal achievements can be written on small pieces of paper and inserted. These achievements: goals, assists, checks, or stick handling successes, once written can be re-read, internalized, and then *owned* to enhance or restore sport confidence.

You might also want to keep a record of 'rewards' you give yourself each time you achieve a personal performance goal. The same can be done for team accomplishments.

11

PEAK PERFORMANCES AND SLUMP BUSTING

A peak performance is that time on the ice when a hockey player is in the flow, when time seems to have slowed down, and when the mind and body are one. The player is 'all there', totally immersed in the ebb and flow of the game. It is this heightened mental and physical state that players strive to achieve, capture and once experienced, to reproduce. Peak performances occur in all sports, and a characteristic of great athletes is that they seem to reach peak performances consistently. Hockey players like Dominique Hasek, Peter Forsberg, Kevin Stevens, and Ray Bourque seem to put game after game together, consistently meeting their goals and expectations. It seems that they know something that can benefit aspiring players. Great hockey players have characteristics in common that allow them to experience frequent peak performances. Let's look at some of these characteristics and see if we can't learn something from them.

CHARACTERISTICS OF PEAK PERFORMERS

Some characteristics shared by top athletes are physical talent, intensity, determination, a powerful drive to win, positive expectations, positive self-talk, specific goal setting skills, the ability to play through pain, and the ability to stay focused in difficult circumstances. In short, they want to be the best, they want not merely to play but to excel. Cynthia Cooper of the WNBA Houston Comets is described by opponents as "incredible - you just can't stop her"! Cynthia wants to be the complete player, "I want to be the best". As a result, she keeps adding new skills to her repertoire, always striving to excel.[38] Peak performances in hockey are most likely to occur when all the conditions are right. By using a mental preparation plan, players can be prepared, relaxed, excited, and in control of factors that contribute to their best performances. In essence, the mental preparation plan tries to ensure that the conditions will be right. Players can then expect good performances. Although today's hockey players don't always have the opportunity for unlimited ice time, they can have the right attitude and use mental practice to accomplish high levels of proficiency.

"Hockey has left the river and never will return. But the river is less a physical place than an attitude, a metaphor for unstructured, unorganized time alone. And if the game no longer needs the place, it still needs the attitude. Without the time it takes just being on the ice, a player is like a student cramming for an exam! The special players like Guy LaFleur have spent time alone with their games, on backyard rinks, in local arenas, time without short cuts. What they have is not an unearned gift!" - Dryden[39]

When learning a new skill, hockey players have to actively concentrate on each step, giving the body directions on where to go and what to do. Eventually, movements are memorized and because of practice, they are speeded up and more sure. Muscle memory takes over during peak performances and the body feels energized and responsive. Some players say that time seems to slow down and the right moves come easily. Peak performance may be thought of as a reward for the hours of physical and mental practice, for it is surely the player's finest hour!

---

[38] Anderson, Kelli. *Sports Illustrated.* September, 1999.

[39] Dryden, Ken. *The Game.* (Penguin Books: New York. 1983) p. 136

Most teams and individual hockey players have experienced a slump or what seems like a long-lasting poor performance period. When this happens players feel unlucky, out of control, and often try to remedy the situation by making drastic changes. A player who can't get the puck in the net will suddenly switch to a stick of a different weight, length, curve, brand, or taping style, often copying the stick choice of a teammate who happens to be on a scoring streak. Players experiencing a slump lose confidence in themselves and in their equipment despite their successes with the same equipment a few weeks or games earlier. Too often, such drastic changes increase an athlete's troubles by adding an adjustment period to the new or modified equipment. The already under-confident player has to adapt to a new stick, hand position, or contact point with the puck. Old superstitions believed to be lucky are discarded and new rituals are tried out of desperation.

When a hockey player is in trouble and can't perform to expectations, one of the first constructive activities is to discuss the problem with the coach who may identify a timing, biomechanical, or strategy problem that could easily be solved. It is also helpful for the player to complete a competition reflection form to identify when, where, and why the problems are occurring. Usually, the problem can be identified and a correction can be made. Fatigue, negative thinking, excess pressure, tension, lack of mental preparation, remarks from a coach, teammate, significant other, or a recent trade can often initiate the loss of the player's confidence and send his or her morale spiraling downhill. Lack of confidence sets the player up for sub par performances which result in more self-imposed pressure, tension, tight muscles, lack of focus, self-doubts →SLUMP! Remember, Gretzky was benched for poor performance and he came out and scored a hat trick! Not all players have those skills, but all can learn to see the situation as a challenge and respond in a productive, constructive manner! As Orlick stated, "The best game within you is who you are!" A great game never just happens. A hockey player never plays over or out of his or her head. If a great game has been played once then it is within the realm of one's physical skills to have it happen again and again but only if it's not pressured, squelched, or negated with self-defeating, negative thoughts.

TO END A SLUMP

1. Restate your goals and reasonable expectations for each practice and game.

2. Reaffirm positive statements about yourself, linemates, and coach.
3. Complete competitive evaluation plans and make minor necessary adjustments to mental preparation plans.

4. Practice 'channel clicking' to turn off negative thoughts.

5. Stay away from other players who think and talk as if they are in slumps. Their comments just reinforce your feelings and the downward spiral continues and accelerates.

6. Treat each drill, practice, and game as very separate entities. Reward yourself for each small success.

7. Prepare for each practice and game using the optimal flow zone chart, ensuring you are neither psyched out nor in need of psych up. Practice keeping yourself in the zone by using the appropriate self-talk, 'I'm excited about tonight's practice, so our line can practice our breakouts', or, 'I'm looking forward to the challenge of winning faceoffs

during that drill.'

8. Put your head totally into each game and practice, shift by shift, and be positive about all accomplishments, no matter how small.

9. Use relaxation and imagery to picture yourself successfully performing the desired skills. If you are unable to <u>see</u> the skill being performed successfully in your mind's eye, then analyze the image to detect where the failure occurs. Play the image slowly, see the error, decide how to correct it, make the correction, and then replay the skill with it executed successfully ... over and over. (If you can see the error and you can't determine how to correct it, talk to your coach or sports counselor.)

10. Play a highlight tape of yourself executing the skill correctly. If you don't have one of yourself, use a video of a player you can identify with who performs the skill the way you want to. Watch it, internalize it, copy it, mentally practice it, and then own it. It belongs to you!

11. Stop thinking or talking about a slump. Instead, just think of it as a time when you haven't achieved your goals.

In conclusion, slump busting is within your power to control. The greats have few slumps. Why? Because they never miss a shot or go without scoring? No! That happens to them, too. But they resist the temptation to make major changes or get down on themselves. They just take a step back, reassess, reset goals, reaffirm their commitment, and go forward into successes. Stay relaxed, focused, have fun, and remember, you are good. It will come!

Excellence is not an act, but a habit -Aristotle

12

TEAM COHESION, SPORTSMANSHIP, AND SOCIAL LOAFING

WHY SOME TEAMS BECOME GREAT

Great teams become great because of a melding of talents and an ability to cooperate and press forward toward a common goal such as the Stanley Cup or a National Championship. The Montreal Canadiens owned the Stanley Cup from 1956-1960 because the talents of Bob Gainey (who G.M.'d the Dallas Stars to a Stanley Cup win in 1999), Larry Robinson, Jacques LeMaire, and Guy LeFleur were combined, with a total team effort. On the other hand, the Chicago Black Hawks of 1961 should have won three straight, considering their talent, but they only ended up with one.[40] This was despite having great players like Bobby Hull, Stan Mikita, and Glenn Hall. Why'? What was missing? When the Edmonton Oilers had to face a play-off series against the defending Stanley Cup Champions, the New York Islanders, Gretzky wrote, "Were we scared'? Petrified! Were we going to show it? No chance." Instead, the Oilers sang on their bench, the entire team chanting, "Here we go Oilers, Here we go." He wrote in his autobiography that "six of us could have still been playing junior hockey and we didn't know how to behave like cool, unflappable, unemotional professionals. We were nervous and jacked up and singing just felt right. Every time we'd get into trouble we would sing. We sang a lot."[41] But they won their first Stanley Cup. They pulled together to face their fear and functioned cohesively as a team.

---

[40] Fischler, Stan. *Golden Ice.* (MacGraw Hill: Scarborough, Ont. 1990) p.221.
[41] Gretzky, Wayne. *An Autobiography.* (Harper Collins Publishers: New York, NY. 1990)

1. Rate your knowledge of Team Cohesion.

1	2	3	4	5
very low				very high

2. Rate your belief about the importance of Team Cohesion.

1	2	3	4	5
very low				very high

3. Rate your plans to promote Team Cohesion.

1	2	3	4	5
very low				very high

Hockey teams developing cohesion must have leadership, team character, and solidarity within the organization. During the developing stage they will strive for stability, trust, and cooperation in an atmosphere where team members can express themselves without fear of rejection. Team cohesion, which literally means 'the sticking together of team members', is assessed by the degree to which a team plays effectively on a consistent basis. Ideally, if a team is cohesive, efforts of the players are directed toward the best interests of the team while individual gains are secondary.

Frequently, coaches are faced with the challenge of bringing individual hockey players together to form a cohesive, cooperative team in a short period of time. Increasingly, from high school onward, teams are formed with players from all across Canada and the United States. In the NHL, players come from the Soviet Union, Sweden, Finland, Czechoslovakia, and North America. Sometimes the players on a team may not even speak the same language. Players on Junior National hockey teams in Canada and the United States are selected from across the continent and within a short amount of time are expected to succeed in competition. In these cases, the challenge is how to quickly create a feeling of family as well as a sense of commitment and caring between players who have previously been strangers. Fortunately, what usually makes their bonding easier is that they share a common goal; having fun and winning, although the constant competition among teammates for playing time, specific linemates, and the coach's confidence should not be overlooked.

For many years we have had a mental toughness program with Junior A hockey teams in the United States Hockey League (USHL). At the beginning and end of most sessions, we use games and initiatives for fun and to promote team cohesion. An abbreviated but similar program was introduced in December, 1990, 1991, and 1992 to the Junior National Hockey teams. Programs have also been implemented with high school, Division I, IHL, and NHL teams. As we become increasingly aware of cohesion and the process of helping individuals evolve into a team, we see that aspects of the program introduced to these teams are based on team or group development theory.

TEAM DEVELOPMENT THEORY

The stages of group development according to Tuckman are: forming, storming, norming, and performing.

1. In the forming stage, hockey players, like members of all groups, usually experience the desire for membership in a group, anger, frustration, confusion, politeness, and superficiality. Emphasis is centered on the 'team' and players frequently talk about 'we'. There are several games and initiatives to expedite the forming stage of team development. The objectives of games and initiatives used in this stage are directed toward breaking the ice, getting acquainted, trust building, and fostering interdependency.

Appropriate to this stage are introduction games such as: animals, the lap sit, yurt circle, trust falls, the trust walk, Power Play (the trivial pursuit game of hockey), the potato game, and the banana race (See Appendix 3 for Games). The adoption of team rituals, quotes, verses, or songs is also encouraged. Involvement in the games promotes camaraderie and fun as well as cohesion among linemates. The 1990-1991 Junior National team coached by Kevin Constantine, Walt Kyle, and Bob "OC" O'Connor had an ongoing competition between lines, keeping track of cumulative points gained from on-ice drills, quizzes at the chalk talks, and off-ice games.

DISCUSSION

At the forming stage level of team development, the leader plays a friendly, directive role. The atmosphere should be one of safety and comfort so as to enable players to express feelings and concerns. The leader must set the tone for risk taking and honesty, encouraging an atmosphere of acceptance. Ideally coaches should participate.

2. In the storming stage of team development, hockey players may be unconsciously struggling with issues of control, power, influence, and decision making. Almost unknowingly, players establish team rules (written and unwritten) and will question and challenge the existing leadership of coaches and captains. It is during the storming stage that a team pecking order is established. Injuries, trades, and frequent line changes can threaten the existing order. This is why both positive and negative consequences must be considered before making trades or other changes that may disrupt the team balance.

The games appropriate to this stage are more complex, thinking-type initiatives such as the electric fence, monster, power play, the 12' wall, and a problem design (See Appendix 3). These games involve working as a team or as a line to solve a particular problem.

Members of the 1991 Jr. National Team: Scott Lachance, Ken Klee, and Brent Brekke catching goalie Mike Dunham, who didn't let them down either in the World Junior Tournament
Reprinted with permission of USA Hockey

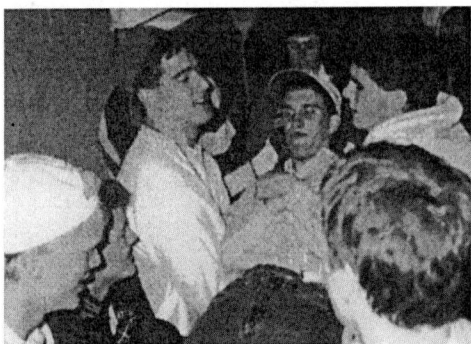

Ted Drury of Harvard in the Potato Race while Trent Klatt and Craig Johnson of the University of Minnesota, Doug Weight of Lake Superior State now with the Edmonton Oilers and Bill Lindsay and Derek Plante wait their turns Reprinted with permission of USA Hockey

The 1991 Jr. National team working together to get all members safely over the 'electric fence.'
Reprinted with permission of USA Hockey

The 1992 bronze medal winning Jr. National Team working to win the group 'egg fall.' Ryan Sittler, Mike Dunham and Cory Saurdiff give advice
Reprinted with permission of USA Hockey

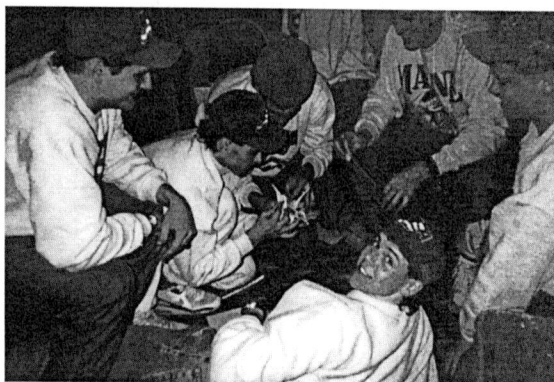

In the electric fence initiative, for example, the team must figure out how to get all of its members over the electric fence without touching it. These initiatives often provide opportunities for communication, problem solving, skill development, and office leadership to emerge. Elements of adversity can be added so players have a real sense of accomplishment and share in the success of their achievement.

DISCUSSION

After each session, teams typically become increasingly group-led and less leader directed. The philosophy, purpose, value, strength, and limitations of the activity just completed and its role in the team's developmental process should be discussed.

3.   The norming stage addresses concerns of leadership and encourages sharing, negotiation, cooperation, and growth.

'NORMING' GAMES AND INITIATIVES

Games and tasks at this stage should be more sophisticated so as to continue to both challenge and unite the group as a whole. The games and initiatives are more complex due to the level of team development and include activities which promote feedback, allow conflict resolution, and stimulate problem design such as the 'all aboard' or 'egg fall'. Examples might be a team participating in planning practices, a new power play, meetings, a youth hockey clinic, a canoe trip, fund raising events, or social occasions like a Christmas party. Team goals are important to all team members.

DISCUSSION

Discussion should focus on constructively evaluating the activities in which the team participated.

4.   The performing stage has been achieved when the team is working independently yet together, when they perform effectively in subgroups (lines). There must be a willingness to cooperate together for what is best for the team and to

support the subgroup's decisions.

DIFFICULTIES

Teams may have real difficulties in moving through these stages of team development. A championship team matures in this process to the point of 'performing' whereas a mediocre team will 'storm' to the point of having to 'reform'. The Dallas Stars looked like a "performing" team during the Stanley Cup. Particularly notable was the unselfish play of Mike Modano who made huge personal sacrifices for the team (played through what should have been a season-ending injury) and Brett Hull who rose to the occasion when needed despite a pulled groin.

One team I worked with during the 1998-99 season started out well but bogged down in "storming" during the fall. They were positioned at a point where they could either develop cohesion and move ahead as a united force or fall behind in fragments. It was a choice! Despite excellent leadership from their captains, the team failed to rally and bowed out early! Often trades are made to try to shake up the team dynamics and to move the team past the storming process. A few years ago, the New York Rangers sought Mark Messier because they believed he had the leadership ability to move a team through the stages to performing. Mark Messier seemed to bring leadership skills to the New York Rangers. This year the Avalanche traded for the Philadelphia Flyer, Shjon Podein, who usually brings a 100% work ethic to the locker room.

GAMES AND INITIATIVES IN APPLICATION

As mentioned earlier, the teams I work with open and close mental toughness meetings by engaging in games and initiatives designed to promote team cohesion. Ideally, these activities accelerate and strengthen camaraderie which, under normal team circumstances, might take a long time to develop. An outstanding team is always more than the sum of its parts. It is likely that strong cohesion among players makes the difference between a good team and a great team. Gretzky noted that while he played for the Edmonton Oilers, the team always enjoyed at least one or two lunches a week together to enhance the togetherness and familiarity among players. Unfortunately, many college, junior, and high school teams cannot create these opportunities to gather together informally. Because off-ice time together is limited by college courses, study programs, and jobs, team meetings and other social occasions must be of maximum quality. It is important to ensure that these sessions are not only instructional but also provide situations that facilitate cohesion and leadership.

It is important that all who work with teams remember that ultimately players are alone on the ice and must feel competent and confident to take control and lead their teammates.

If hockey players are constantly in subordinate, student type roles during team meetings and activities, then they are not getting practice in doing anything but following directions. It is important to stimulate leadership opportunities and allow positive behaviors, such as creativity and initiative, to develop off the ice so that players will be more likely to demonstrate these same traits on the ice. All teams need lots of leaders, not just captains; every player must try to step forward, take some risks, and contribute to keeping the team motivated, focused, and cohesive.

When hockey players are involved in off-ice games that require trust, mutual problem solving, and physical or emotional risk, the bond that they create may translate into improved on-ice performance. For example, helping each other blindfolded through an outdoor maze on a frozen lake at night, which requires trust in your partner, may transfer into a trust that your partner will help you on-ice to free up the puck in the corner.

It is essential upon completion of a game or initiative, that the exercise is analyzed and the principles of the exercise are applied to hockey! The discussions about a particular exercise should focus upon making analogies between that activity and the aspect of hockey to which the lessons apply. Furthermore, these games and initiatives can often be applied to life situations beyond the hockey arena wherever they are found appropriate.

A Junior team I worked with was successful in winning the USHL Championship, two of the several years we have had the mental toughness program. Clearly, on-ice factors are the most important, but when talent and hard work are combined with a sense of cohesion (teamwork, enthusiasm, and leadership, on and off-ice), the combination may be unbeatable.

In the best case scenario, team players should like each other so that *esprit de corps* (team spirit) can develop, which may improve the chances that a team will win. Ron Hextall, when describing the two goals he scored in the NHL as a goaltender, said, "the biggest thing was when my teammates came over the boards and were so excited. That was such a big thrill, the way they responded. It was a moment for myself and a highlight of my career. They could have said, Big Deal. But they were screaming all around me, and I remember being in the middle of the pile thinking, 'What did we do, win the Stanley Cup?'" In Hextall's case, the team turned an individual's personal success into a reason for celebrating which further promoted the team cohesion.

THE JUNIOR NATIONAL HOCKEY TEAM-1991

For Kevin Constantine, the coach of the Junior National Hockey Team in 1990-1991, the biggest challenge was how to establish cohesion among players in a very short amount of time. Players were selected from rivaling teams in Division I hockey and within less than two weeks he was to have the team ready to face the USSR and Team Canada in the opening round of the World Junior Tournament. This challenge was discussed and it was decided to emphasize sport psychology skills to help the athletes maintain positive self-talk, manage stress, promote positive expectations, and accelerate team camaraderie and cohesion.

PROGRAM IMPLEMENTED

During his early contact with the team at Colorado Springs, the coach created positive expectancy about the 'Mental Toughness' sessions scheduled. The sessions were designed to be both dynamic and upbeat. The forming stage was started by having players introduce themselves, their college, their on-ice positions, and name a favorite activity. It became clear that loyalty among subunits had already formed when players began to introduce themselves by telling which line Constantine had assigned them to. They had already started to identify themselves with their on-ice linemates and each line found its own nickname. A friendly competition between lines had been deliberately planned to foster and accelerate their bonding.

Following the introduction exercise we reviewed the goals and overall agenda for the Mental Toughness sessions. We introduced motivation theory, goal setting, optimal flow zone, arousal level, relaxation, and psyching up techniques, attribution theory, positive self-talk, channel clicking, and finally, social loafing theory. The games and initiatives we employed were the "balloon-pop" as a way to destroy negative emotions, the "trust fall" to foster a sense of trust among the players and coaches, and the "electric fence" which requires initiative, planning, problem solving, and trust. The "potato game", which fosters fun and foolishness thereby breaking down barriers, and the "yurt circle", which promotes interdependence, were also included. The Power Play trivia game was played to promote competition between lines, cohesion among the linemates, and test comprehension of hockey information found in off-ice chalk talks and on-ice sessions.

SETTING LINES EARLY

From the standpoint of team cohesion, I think there are some major advantages to setting lines early and letting them gel. Athletes who have to coordinate motor skills with other teammates do best when they have the opportunity to work together over a period of time. Knowing each other's speed and habits enables a player to anticipate what his or her teammate might do. This allows the well-oiled line to gain an advantage over opponents. The best team players seem to be able to sense where each other will be and what each other will do before it happens. I think that is partly why teams sometimes pay a lot of money to reunite players such as Teemu Selanne and Paul Kariya. University of Minnesota Gopher Hockey fans will recall watching Neal and Paul Broten and Butsy Erickson leave opponents looking for their jock straps as they put on exhibitions of the most intricate passing game. The same was true when the San Jose Sharks reunited Igor Larianov and Sergei Makarov, players from the Soviet National Team. Their finesse helped the Sharks advance to the second round of the Stanley Cup playoffs. Years of playing together has advantages that often over-compensate for lack of physical ability.

Watching the Junior National team quickly form sub-groups that could be cohesive within the structure of the team reinforced my belief that whenever possible in hockey, this should occur. The defensemen, center, and wings paired up and learned a lot about each other on and off the ice. This accelerated their adjustment and fueled their intensity to do well as a line. Lines performing well contribute to a successful, winning, team effort. As mentioned earlier, this Junior National team had the best performance of any team in their age group in 15 years. Many of the players from this team were invited to the second tryout camp of the 1992 Olympic Team. The following year a similar philosophy was implemented by Coach Walt Kyle and the Junior National team won a bronze medal in the World Junior Tournament.

Naturally, if a line isn't working out, the coach will make adjustments. Should that happen, players must learn to transfer their loyalties quickly to new linemates in order to optimize the likelihood of the new line succeeding.

Unfortunately, too often players pout when they are moved "down" a line. Little do they know that it is often said that the quality of the fourth line will determine who wins the Stanley Cup!

SELF-TEST 7:2

1. Rate your knowledge of Team Cohesion.

1	*2*	*3*	*4*	*5*
very low				*very high*

2. Rate Your belief about the importance of Team Cohesion.

1	*2*	*3*	*4*	*5*
very low				*very high*

3. Rate your plans to promote Team Cohesion.

1	2	3	4	5
very low				*very high*

SOCIAL LOAFING: PUTTING AN "I" IN TEAM!

One difficulty in hockey is having all members of a hockey team putting out their maximum efforts simultaneously. Individual players who fail to play at 100% effort may be accused of social loafing! Research in sport psychology shows that if a Tug of War occurs, groups will pull with more force than individuals but not with as much force as would be predicted from summing the individual scores. Eight persons do not pull 8 times harder than one individual, they only pull 4 times as hard. This is called the 'Ringelmann effect'. Two persons will pull with 93% of the individual effort, 3 persons pull at 85%, and 8 persons pull at 49% of individual effort. It is scary to think what percent of individual effort a hockey team plays at when it has close to 20 players. It is believed that motivation drops off as group size increases because the responsibility is spread out or diffused.

SOCIAL LOAFING

What causes social loafing and how does it relate to hockey'? One reason for social loafing is that players may assume that others perform with less effort when in groups and they consequently reduce their own effort. It is also possible that players save their maximum efforts for the more individualized conditions, when they are the most identifiable, such as when they are on the power play or on a man short. These are situations in which they are likely to receive more individual attention. It is believed that identifiability of individual performance is critical and when individual efforts are lost in the crowd, performance decreases.

STRATEGIES *TO REDUCE SOCIAL LOAFING*

1. Coaches usually monitor individual performances which can lessen social loafing. This is done in hockey by keeping track of plus/minus, points, effectiveness etc.

2. Recognizing individual behaviors that contribute to group performance and providing positive feedback is helpful. This improves performance more than feedback only on group performance.

3. Simple verbal encouragement (from a coach who is really respected by players) in recognition of performance is often more effective in increasing motivation than extrinsic rewards.

Current literature suggests that professional, college, high school, and youth hockey coaches who recognize individual efforts within teams may well have more effective teams than those who reward only group performance outcomes and downplay individual performances. The old saying that there is no I in TEAM has some obvious merit, but I say there is an I in team and it stands for *Identifiability.*

CONTRIBUTING TO TEAM COHESION

It is extremely important that all hockey players take responsibility to promote team effectiveness and cohesion.

1. Teams should expect to have fun together and enjoy each other as a group.

2. Players should neither downplay nor overstate their own

talents. Let your performance speak for itself. After all, actions speak louder than words.

3. Play up to your potential, always striving to meet challenging but realistic goals. Compare yourself only to the goals you set for yourself.

4. If you are successful, be generous in praise to linemates for their checks and passes that helped you make the good play, but only if it is sincere.

5. If you do receive recognition or publicity from the coach or media, accept it quietly, internalize it, and allow it to further your own drive to master the sport.

6. Remember success and media attention is distracting and short lived so take it in stride.

7. Think not only of yourself, but also of helping your linemates reach their goals. However, your assistance must never be to the extent that you fail to do what is best to win the game.

8. Sometimes players want so much to be liked that they fear being puck hogs and pass constantly instead of taking the opportunity to shoot. If it's there, go for it! As Coach Kaufman, of the Rochester Mustangs says, "It can be selfish not to shoot"[42] You don't meet anyone's goals if a puck is being aimlessly passed around.

9. Remember the concept of social loafing. Try to always perform up to the best of your ability. Lots of the top players rise above the others by reaching to achieve their own goals even when playing on a team that is not

---

[42] Kaufman, Mark. Ideas for goal setting for hockey players, 1990.

performing well. You may also help pull your team up! Let them chase you for awhile!

10. Team goals are best met when each player considers his contribution to be important, recognizable, and helpful in contributing to the team effort of winning the game!

SPORTSMANSHIP

The best players I have known have exemplified the principles of good sportsmanship. It is said that the cream always rises to the top. Class players are to be revered, for they contribute to the speed and flow of a game requiring great skill. As mentioned earlier, a Junior A team I worked with won the National Championship at the same time they won the award for the best sportsmanship. The next year, I saw many cheap penalties and they won neither the championship, nor the sportsmanship award. Players who play their game in a disciplined manner and can avoid taking cheap shots at other players enhance the likelihood that the game plan can be achieved. Players who constantly force their team to play a man short lessen the effectiveness of the team. There is no status in taking penalties (except in the NHL at which level intimidation is paramount). For the most part, penalties are usually too costly in terms of goals given up when there is a player in the penalty box. Hockey players who role model the best skills of the game offer a viable legacy to the youngsters in hockey who will follow. These players will succeed because their focus will be on speed and skill rather than on senseless penalty taking. As it was written when the Edmonton Oilers won the Stanley Cup, "The sleek shall inherit the ice." This was evident again in the 1992 Olympics when the unified team won the Gold Medal. The best team won despite a good effort by the Canadian Team. This does not mean that defense in hockey is not important. It is, but play a clean, hard checking game that can keep all your players on the ice and out of the penalty box. There is a strong correlation between good sportsmanship and good teams. The 1992 Olympic Gold medal was won by the Unified Team which appeared skilled, disciplined, and in control. Dave King's Team Canada won the silver and also demonstrated discipline and skill. The 1992 Junior National Team, coached by Walt Kyle, John Conniff, and O.C. O'Connor won a bronze medal in the World Junior Tournament. One of their goals was to be the least penalized team. They only missed that goal by one penalty and they won the first medal a U.S. team had taken in 16 years of World Junior competition. There is usually a strong link between winning and mental discipline. The following Appendix provides a brief description of many games and team building exercises that add fun to team meetings and promote team cohesion.

Appendix 3

Games[43] and Initiatives for Cohesion

ANIMALS- The team selects 5 animals they would like to see imitated. The names of the animals selected are written out 5 times and put in a hat. Players each draw the name of an animal, close their eyes, and when the game begins they must try to imitate the animal in noise and actions. Each 'animal' must find his own species and collect in a group with the object being that the first group to find all of its members wins. The last animal to find his group loses and is given a small task to do. If there are only 20 players, four species of animals will suffice.

LAPSIT- The team stands with shoulders touching in

---

[43] New Games-Outward Bound Education Exercises

a circle. Players then all turn to the right and sit back on each other's laps. Then in a coordinated fashion, all players move their right legs, then their left, etc. In this synchronized fashion, the players scoot along on the floor moving as a caterpillar. This exercise requires cooperation, coordination, and through its close physical proximity among players, it increases player to player bonding and team cohesion.

YURT CIRCLE -The team stands in a circle and numbers off: 1, 2, 1, 2, etc. Then all hold hands and the leader calls "Ones IN, Two's OUT." The players hold hands and lean in opposite directions while supported by their opposite numbers. This exercise reminds players that a team is only as strong as its weakest link.

TRUST FALL- *This exercise, due to its risk factor, should only be done with a leader who has supervised this exercise before.

POTATO GAME- Teams can be divided into lines or groups of equal size. Chairs are placed at one end of the room. At the opposite end buckets are placed on the floor for the potatoes to be dropped into. A potato is placed on each of the chairs. Competing teams are lined up like relay teams. The starters have to sit down on the chairs and pick up the potatoes between their legs without ever using their hands. Then they race to the other end and by straddling the bucket the potato is dropped in. If it lands in the bucket, the player can pick it up and run it back, setting it on the chair for his teammate to start. If the potato is dropped in route to the bucket or misses the pail, the player must return to his chair and start over. The first relay team to complete the race wins.

POWER PLAY -This game is a form of trivial pursuit, using the 'power puck' (a wheel of fortune) that gets spun, and tests knowledge of categories such as sport psychology, sports physiology, sports nutrition, sports medicine, and sport trivia. Each coach or sport psychology counselor can make up their own inventory of questions, although an example is provided at the end of the chapter.

ELECTRIC FENCE- A piece of string or rope is tied between 2 objects at about shoulder height. The object is to get all members of the team over the 'electric fence' without getting anyone electrocuted. A 6 foot plank of about 6 inches in width is usually the only available prop. This exercise is designed to have players work out a strategy that will allow them to get all of their members over, even the last man. *This is also best done in the presence of an experienced leader.

PASS THE PUCK- This exercise is a team goal setting drill. It is simple and fun while demonstrating the effectiveness of communication and goal setting. Use a small black puck-shaped bean bag about the size of a softball, a ball, or whatever is available. Have players start by standing in a circle. Give 'the puck' to one player. The player chosen is to pass (throw) it to anyone else in the circle and remember who it was passed to and the player who catches it must remember who passed it to him. Each member of the team can only pass it once. Once begun, the exercise should be timed to see how long it takes for the puck to be passed once to each member. The players are then told that they don't have to remain in a circle to perform the exercise. The object is to see if the team can improve upon their time by forming a new arrangement. This exercise uses goal setting because the team consistently tries to improve upon its old time by organizing themselves in a manner that will allow for a faster hand off or pass to the adjacent player. Soon the players quickly figure out the alignment of players that is the fastest arrangement where they can hand the pass off quickly.

When goals are clearly stated, as in Pass the Puck game, by trying to improve upon a previous time, creative strategies must be devised to realize these goals. This encourages contributions from some off-ice rather than on-ice leaders. Usually the more cognitive players benefit as they will see the answers faster and gain new confidence among better on-ice players. This exercise has applications to hockey, not unlike the quick passing drills used on the 'Power Play.'

TRANSITIONS (CLOTHES PINS) - Stand players in a circle, one behind the other with right shoulders facing in. The instructor stands in the center of a circle and gives one clothes pin to each player. Each player then pins one to the back of the player in front of him. The game begins with a whistle and the goal is to get the clothespin off of other players' backs while protecting one's own. No pushing or tripping is allowed but players can run, move quickly, turn, spin, etc. Whistles can be used as in shifts, so players can stop, reset goals, and continue on the next whistle. The last one to survive with his clothes pin on Wins. You can also reward players who collect the highest number of clothes pins before getting out.

The benefits of this exercise are creativity, quickness on transition, and moves. At first, some players assume a defensive posture and will back against the wall to protect their pins. Others might ask where to put all the clothes pins they get, revealing real positive expectancy and offensive orientation. The most important lesson for hockey might be the discussion that follows this game. It is important to recognize which strategies are effective, such as speed in transition from offense to defense (i.e., "I want his pin, but I don't want him to get mine," is similar to "I want to put the puck in his net, but I won't let him put the puck in mine"). Overall, this is a quick little game which makes some important points that you might want to discuss with your team afterward.

BANANA GAME- The banana game is a fun relay race in which ideally the team is divided into five lines of five players. For example, 2 forwards, a center, and a pair of defense who usually play together on-ice can join forces for the relay. A forward line can also join forces with a goalie or odd-man player to quickly form a unit.

The five relay teams line up and each lead-off player is handed a banana. All relay teams are seated on the floor behind their lead-off player. Lead-off players pass the banana, which is held in the feet, behind by rolling up backwards to where the number two player receives the banana in a foot-off (instead of a hand-off) and repeats the sequence, etc. When the last player receives the banana, the player spins around and passes it back to the player it was received from and the sequence continues until the banana is received by the lead-off player. The lead-off player quickly peels the banana and stuffs it in his mouth.

The winning team is the one who follows the sequence and is the first to show the banana has disappeared as instructed.

POWER PLAY

INSTRUCTIONS: Divide into four teams, each team with a captain. Two teams go with one coach while the other two teams go with the other coach. You need to adapt questions to level of participation and to the principles you want to emphasize. Make two spin wheels (paper plates, markers, arrow to spin/tack). If this is not possible, a dice can be tossed. The value of the toss will indicate the number of points earned if the question is correctly answered.

Questions are based upon:

- PHYSIOLOGY OF ICE HOCKEY

- PSYCHOLOGY OF ICE HOCKEY

- BIOMECHANICS OF ICE HOCKEY

- HOCKEY STRATEGY AND HISTORY

- HOCKEY TRIVIA

The coach will spin the arrow and the number of points nearest to where it stops is the value of the question. The coach will read the question and allow a maximum of 30 seconds for the team to discuss and decide on an answer. The captain will answer for the team and if the answer is correct, the team gets the points. If the answer is wrong, the correct answer will be read and the opposing team gets their turn. Each team must answer questions from each category. The winning teams play each other in a championship round.

QUESTIONS FOR POWER PLAY

Team A, C

Team B, D

PHYSIOLOGY OF HOCKEY

PHYSIOLOGY OF HOCKEY

1. Hockey is both aerobic and anaerobic (uses both of those energy systems) TRUE

1. Good aerobic conditioning will enable a player to recover his oxygen debt faster after a shift TRUE

2. The average % body fat is about 5-6% in the NHL. FALSE the average is 12-13% - Gretzky is 14%. Hockey players need some body fat to cover vital organs.

2. Hockey does not cause excessive sweating and loss of fluids. FALSE Hockey players lose lots of fluids - very important to drink lots of water (2000 cc per day over and above estimated fluid loss during practices or games).

1. All players on a team should prepare "mentally" for a game in the same way so the team is aroused to the same level? FALSE, Some players calm down to play their best and others need to "psych up." In the locker room, respect your teammates uniqueness.

2. During "a peak performance" hockey players often feel everything is automatic, going with the flow. We call this being in the "optimal flow zone." TRUE. During a peak performance, players are mentally in the game and nowhere else.

PSYCHOLOGY OF HOCKEY

1. Imagery is most effective if it follows relaxation as the mind is cleared during relaxation of all thoughts except a focus on the breathing. TRUE Clearer images occur after relaxation.

2. "Goal Setting" is not effective for a hockey player. Just trying to do my best is enough. FALSE- Research shows that athletes who take goal setting seriously improve more, perform better, and experience less anxiety.

BIOMECHANICS OF ICE HOCKEY

1. Hockey involves short phases of acceleration and deceleration. So many drills should be of high intensity and short duration. TRUE

2. Most hockey players have excellent abdominal strength. FALSE. The abdominal strength of most hockey players is very weak. Hockey players should strengthen abdominal muscles to help support the back.

BIOMECHANICS OF ICE HOCKEY

1. To accelerate fast which statements are true?
(a) increase knee flexion
(b) increase forward lean of trunk
(c) increase stride rate
TRUE

2. During a body check a hockey player may stop breathing for a second to perform the "isometric contraction" necessary to forcefully check. This breath hold may affect the player's oxygen level and tire him faster. TRUE

HOCKEY STRATEGIES AND HISTORY

1. Coaches like players' sticks up off the ice around the "net" in the "offensive zone" so that they can "bat pass" the puck to their linemate. <u>FALSE.</u> He wants the sticks on the ice

2. Mental Toughness also refers to the mental discipline needed to avoid unnecessary penalties <u>TRUE</u>

<u>Reasons</u>
(a) We put their best players out on their power play (b) Penalties and unnecessary roughness distract "skill" players from their game and this is a skilled disciplined team

HOCKEY STRATEGIES AND HISTORY

1. When you take a penalty:
(a) your team comes off the offensive
(b) your team is vulnerable to be scored on.
(c) the "man short lines" are then tired and are especially vulnerable the first minute after. <u>TRUE</u>

2. This team must work even harder now for the rest of the season on cohesion, working hard, staying focused, and having fun! <u>TRUE</u> Stay <u>humble</u> and <u>generous</u> to teammates. You are all of equal importance and necessary to the success of the team. The only "I" in team is identifiability.

TRIVIA

1. During the 1999 NHL season, Dallas Stars coach, Ken Hitchcosk, scheduled a total of four practices in February and March to keep the team fresh. The coach said that over the past two years the players have come to understand the huge emotional commitment that needs to be made and they pushed themselves. <u>TRUE</u>

1. It is said of Gretzky that "The Great One made a career out of shining brightest when the most eyes were on him." <u>TRUE.</u> Sports Illustrated, April 1999.

2. When the Dallas Stars won the Stanley Cup in 1999, beating the Buffalo Sabres, the Stanley Cup ring goalie Ed Belfour received was one of many he has won over the years. <u>FALSE.</u> The Stanley Cup win for the Dallas Stars in 1999 was Ed Belfour's first.

2. Even though Gretzky scored 894 goals before he retired, Gretzky said he'll be remembered best for his passing. <u>TRUE.</u> Sports Illustrated, April 1999.

The content of the 'Power Play' game must constantly be updated to ensure that material is current, accurate, and consistent with the coaches' and sport counselor's philosophy.

CHAMPIONSHIP GAME OF

"POWER PLAY"

PHYSIOLOGY

1. Short shifts help prevent a build up of lactic acid. If the shift is intense it should be short. <u>TRUE</u>

1. Anaerobic exercise in hockey means skating with an oxygen supply. <u>FALSE.</u> Anaerobic means without oxygen.

PSYCHOLOGY

1. Your teammates play better when their self-esteem is low - they will try harder. It helps them when you and the coach yell at them. <u>FALSE.</u> Athletes and non-athletes perform best when they feel good about themselves. Praise that is sincere helps.

2. "Channel Clicking" is a form of "negative thought stopping" to help control the negative self-talk that goes on in players' heads after they have been criticized, benched, or have made a mistake. Channel Clicking is important because success follows positive thoughts. <u>TRUE</u>

BIOMECHANICS

1. Hockey players hit and are hit by 200 lb. objects (other players) who are travelling at speeds upward of 25 mph. <u>TRUE</u>

1. In hockey conditioning, the components include aerobic (heart and lungs), anaerobic (explosive action), and strength training along with rest and relaxation. <u>TRUE</u>

2. "Negativity" can be helpful to your teammates. If you repeatedly comment on your linemates faults eventually they will get it right. <u>FALSE.</u> Hockey teams get enough "correction" from their coaches. The role of a teammate is to be totally supportive and noncritical of each other.

2. It's better to hold back a little speed and finesse in practice and "save it" for the game. <u>FALSE.</u> To train and improve the aerobic and anaerobic systems the player must practice as hard as they will play in a game.

TRIVIA

1. Currently (1999) it is said that Pittsburgh Penguin Jaromir Jagr is the most gifted player in the league. <u>TRUE</u>

1. The 1999 Stanley Cup final was won by the Dallas Stars because the Buffalo Sabres goalie, Dominique Hasek, played poorly in goal. <u>FALSE.</u> Hasek played extremely well. The final game was won during the third overtime on a questionable goal.

13

COACH AND PLAYER RELATIONSHIPS

A critical factor in a team or player's success is the relationship between the hockey player and the coach. Ideal relationships are variable and subject to individual characteristics, philosophies, and preferences of both coach and athlete. One Division I hockey player once said to me, "I really play best for a coach I'm prepared to die for. The kind of coach that, if the tables were turned, would put it all out for me and for the team." While that might be extreme, many players I've talked to admit they have had coaches they respect so much that they deliver extraordinary effort to earn the respect of the coach. Others seem ambivalent about their player-coach relationships. Gretzky said of Glen Sather, the long time coach of Edmonton, "I respect Glen Sather as one of the best hockey minds I've been around, but our relationship was getting touchy. He didn't think I should have limits. If I got four goals, he'd be on my butt for not getting five. I guess that was Slat's way of motivating me but it's too bad he never learned that type of thing doesn't motivate me. Everybody's different."[44] Perhaps, Gretzky was better understood by Mike Keenan, who coached Wayne in the 1987 and 1991 Canada Cups and in 1996 with the St. Louis Blues. "His passion to be the best player in the world is what drove him," said Keenan. In sport psychology terms it could be said that Gretzky's strong "intrinsic" motivation likely negated the effect of extrinsic motivation such as Slats was applying.

---

[44] Gretzy, Wayne. *An Autobiography*. (Harper-Collins Publishers: New York. 1990)

MOTIVATION

A brief discussion of motivation is appropriate here as it is important that both coach and player understand what drives players to seek excellence on the ice and beyond! There are many theories of motivation but the most easily understood and applicable to hockey is Maslow's Hierarchy of Needs.

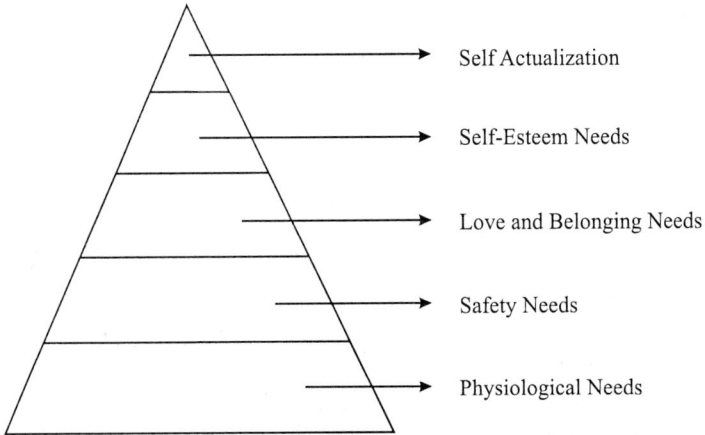

Maslow believed that human beings are motivated initially to satisfy basic *physiological* drives: our appetites for food, thirst, and sex. Once these needs are met, we seek *safety.* This entails protecting ourselves from threats such as injury, illness, flood, freezing, and fire. When assured of safety, humans are motivated by a need for *love and belonging.* Most people need to be accepted in a social group such as a family or perhaps a team. The next drive is for *self-esteem,* the need to be recognized and respected. According to Maslow, only when these drives are satisfied can we really expect to self-actualize and become all that we can be!

APPLICATION OF MASLOW TO HOCKEY

Competitive hockey players face a continual series

of situations that threaten their own hierarchy of needs. The need for physical safety is often challenged by the game itself, with its speed, collisions, sticks, flying pucks, and the emphasis on physical and mental courage and toughness. The need for love and belonging is threatened by frequent changes in teammates, linemates, roommates, traveling, and trades. Changes made by the coach may undermine a player's security or sense of love and belonging. Criticism from coaches, the media, and significant others can be devastating to a player's self-esteem. Putting oneself and one's best effort out there to be evaluated is always scary and threatens self-esteem. According to Maslow, when our needs are satisfied we are most free to achieve all that we desire. Meeting emotional and psychological needs allows a player's motivation to move toward self-actualization. For the hockey player, self-actualization translates into consistency in obtaining optimal or peak performances.

Most players need to feel part of the team, feel secure with their teammates, and believe the coach likes and respects them before they can play their best. A study done on 10,000 school children determined that boys who were involved in team sports ranked their reasons for being involved in the following order of preference: (1) to have fun, (2) to improve skills, (3) for the excitement of competition, (4) to do something I'm good at, (5) to stay in shape, (6) for the challenge of competition, (7) to be part of a team, (8) to win, (9) to go to a higher level of competition, and (10) to get exercise. Usually, having fun, which is the primary motivator, is related to the idea of being with and enjoying peers. And so the study shows that the most important need to have satisfied before reaching peak performance is being accepted and loved by peers, which in hockey relates to friends, teammates, and the coach. Hockey players' off-ice relationships with friends and family, at school and at work, also affect self-esteem and will influence on-ice performance.

If these off-ice relationships are positive, usually the hockey player's overall self-esteem becomes stronger, and on-ice performances benefit. However, if the player's relationships are negative, or are giving him negative feedback about himself, his self-esteem goes down resulting in a decline of on-ice performance. There is not always a direct correlation between self-esteem and performance, but they are related a large majority of the time. The stronger the self-esteem, the better position a player is in, mentally and emotionally, to turn in a top performance.

POWER OF THE COACH

The coach has tremendous power to optimize performance by nurturing the player's hierarchy of needs. A coach who threatens, ridicules, and talks trades forces the athlete to regress back to a lower level of needs. It is similar to gearing down in a car. The athlete who suffers low self-esteem, who is not playing well, and who receives criticism may become preoccupied with trying to justify self-worth. Going back to our analogy of the car, the athlete is unable to reach fourth gear because *of* being stuck in first or second. This athlete is unlikely to have the courage during such an emotional low to take risks, such as seizing the puck, skating with it, making a good move, or taking a great shot. These players, if in fact they must skate and carry the puck, are far more likely to pass because they will not feel the confidence necessary within themselves to take risks or get the job done.

Coaches must understand what Gretzky meant when he said, "A team isn't simply made up of sticks, pucks, and skates, but is a collection of people and the magic between the people has to be just right." Coaches who understand this can work to promote individual players' self-worth and sense of affiliation. A player treated with respect is likely to respond with the I'd-die-out-there-for-the-coach-effort needed when a game has gone into its second overtime and exhaustion begins to set in. Some aspects of coaching style are developmental and, although some "in your face" coaches are tough at the outset, once they see the behavior changes the players or team need, they back off and stop riding the players, satisfied they have established a mutually respectful relationship. Ken Hitchcock, coach of the Dallas Stars (Stanley Cup winners in 1999) said of his team, "Over the past two years they've come to understand the huge emotional commitment that needs to be made. This team judges itself realistically with a harsh appraisal and there is little need for a coach's critique now."

FEEDBACK

Players may still require frequent feedback to tell them whether alterations of their on-ice behaviors are sufficient, not enough, or too much. Because players cannot see themselves in relationship to other players, they may feel they are playing too aggressively, too calmly, or may perceive themselves to be Charlie hustle, when in fact is only 50% of the change the coach wanted. Videotapes are helpful to show where the player is in relation to another player or in relation to the behavior the coach wants executed. Players who believe they have performed optimally and to the best of their ability deserve feedback on why they weren't picked, dressed, or played. There is nothing worse than doing one's best and then receiving no feedback. This situation leaves the player without control since they cannot be sure about what they did wrong or right. Mutual respect demands that coaches meet with their players and give feedback that is constructive and provides a blueprint for the on-ice behaviors that the coach wants to see changed. The ultimate challenge for a coach is to foster an environment which challenges, rewards, and allows for the fullest growth of the players!

Research on the impact of the coach on a player's self esteem can be summarized in one important statement. **Winning and losing do not have as powerful an effect on players' self esteem as the players' perception of how they are valued by the coach.** Whether the team wins or loses, the coach's feedback to players will shape the players' self-perceptions. If the coach remains positive, optimistic, and goal directed, rewarding what was good and constructively addressing what needs changing, players will respond in kind. Even the best coaches struggle when their team is not winning. Unless they are very mature, coaches often have the temptation to point the finger of blame away from themselves. The mature coach who takes the heat will earn their players' loyalty and respect. The following quote is another favorite of hockey sage, Ken Johannson, and illustrates this point most aptly:

I have yet to find a man, however exalted his station, who did not do better work and put forth better effort under a spirit of approval than under a spirit of criticism - Charles Schwab

THE COACH-PLAYER RELATIONSHIP

During the selection process of drafts, tryout camps, and so on, the coaches and hockey players need to be very honest with each other. The coaches must clearly spell out the roles they have in mind for the players and the players must listen to what their coaches say. **Not just what they want to hear!** If, for example, a player is assigned to be a defensive wing but his dream is to be the lead scorer, either the player or the coach will be very unhappy. Families and significant others may encourage a player to accept an offer, believing that the player will become what he wants to be. While this is possible, it is important to trust that the coach is a good judge of ability and probably has the player accurately evaluated. If the player is happy with the role on the team offered at the outset of the season, then both the player's goals and the coach's goals will be congruent. This is necessary for the beginning of a good relationship. Good communication, discussion of mutual goals, and constructive feedback is imperative if the relationship between coach and player is to flourish. Trust and confidentiality is a two-way street and must be the backbone of any good relationship between players and coaches.

**If you treat an individual as he is, he will stay that way,
but if you treat him as if he were what he could be,
he will become what he could be – Goethe**

Can I really trust these players after the way I worked them?
Kevin Constantine demonstrated that he is one of the best when he took over coaching responsibilities for the San Jose Sharks and led the team to the second round of the Stanley Cup Playoffs (1994). He is currently coaching the Pittsburgh Penguins and will coach a team to a Stanley Cup win during his career. He is shown here doing the trust fall (1990-1991).
Reprinted with permission of USA Hockey

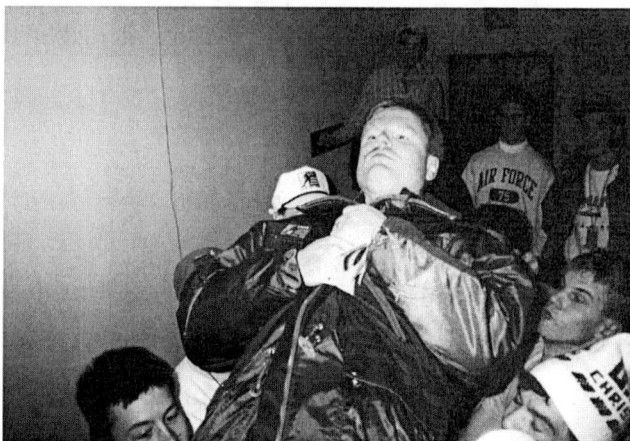

Chapter 14, Sports Medicine, is written by Dr. Michael J. Stuart who has both professional and personal interest in ice hockey. He has been an investigator on many USA hockey studies and he has been the physician for youth, high school, Junior A, USA National, and Olympic teams for over a decade. Mike is a former football player and is now the proud parent of 4 children, all of whom excel in ice hockey. His eldest son, Mike, is a sophomore defenseman at Colorado College and has played on National Junior teams. Colin is a senior in high school and a talented center with the USHL - Junior A team in Lincoln, Nebraska. Mark, also an exceptional athlete, is playing high school football and hockey for Lourdes High School. Cristin, an 8th grader, plays for the John Marshall girls high school hockey team. Wife and mother, Nancy Stuart, has served as team manager to many of the Stuart childrens' teams and effectively coordinates the family activities.

Dr. Stuart and his son, Mike, are pictured below.

14

SPORTS MEDICINE

Michael J. Stuart, M.D.

Injuries in ice hockey tend to increase as players mature. Characteristics of ice hockey that contribute to injuries include the high-speed motion, the rigid, unyielding boards, a slippery surface, and potentially dangerous equipment such as sticks, skates, and puck. Understanding the cause, type, and severity of injuries is essential to minimize these risks. The 'macho' image of the seasoned hockey player with numerous facial scars and no front teeth is a thing of the past.

INCIDENCE

A higher injury rate is associated with increased age, skill, and size of the players. The hours of practice or play per injury change dramatically according to the level of competition. A study of amateur hockey players showed that 100 hours of practice or play transpired for each injury in the 5-14 year-old age group; whereas among the professionals, an injury occurred every 7 hours.[45]

Level of Participation	Hours of Practice or Play per Injury
YOUTH	100
HIGH SCHOOL	16
COLLEGE	11
PROFESSIONAL	7

---

[45] Sutherland, GW. Fire on Ice "American Journal of Sports Medicine". 4: 264-269, 1976.

The injury rate for a youth hockey player in a year was 0.02 compared to a professional player who had an injury rate of 3.0 per year. Factors which contribute to this discrepancy include the increased player size and speed, lack of protective equipment (face mask), frequent collision forces resulting from body checking, and tolerance of illegal activities such as fighting. Approximately 75 percent of injuries occur during games with only 25 percent occurring during practices, which probably reflects the higher intensity of competition.

During the 1994-5 and 1995-6 seasons, USA Hockey undertook a prospective observational analysis of ice hockey players in nine communities in the United States at seven different levels of competition (unpublished data). The incidence of injury was calculated by converting the number of injuries during games and practices into 1,000 hours of estimated playing time. Injuries were very infrequent among the Mite and Squirt players, but a similar rate increase was identified for the Peewee, Bantam, and Midget players. High School athletes were at the greatest risk in the population studied.

Table 1. Injury number and rate by level of participation

Division	Injuries per 1,000 hours		
	Practice	Game	Total
Mite* (n=2)	1.0	0.0	0.8
Squirt (n=10)	0.2	2.7	0.6
Peewee (n=44)	1.4	12.1	3.8
Bantam (n=32)	0.6	11.8	3.0
Midget# (n=5)	2.6	9.0	4.6
High School# (n=9)	2.7	31.1	9.3
Seniors# (n=2)	0.0	6.8	6.8
Total (n=102)	0.7	7.8	2.2

*Mites: 1995-96 only

#Midget, High School, and Seniors 1994-95 only

The risk of injury in a game was significantly higher than in practice for the squirt, peewee, bantam and high school players (p<0.001). The rate ratio (increased risk) of game injury compared to practice injury was 15 for Squirts, 9 for Peewees, 20 for Bantams, and 12 for High School players.

CAUSES OF INJURY

High speeds obtained by players, sticks, and pucks along with the need for abrupt acceleration and deceleration contribute to the occurrence of injuries. Skating velocities of 30 mph for senior amateur players and 20 mph for peewee players have been recorded. Players are especially vulnerable when sliding on the ice at speeds up to 15 mph because of the decreased ability to decelerate and protect themselves before hitting the boards or another player. The mechanism of injury following these high-speed collisions is usually from *contact* with another player, the boards, net, or ice. Serious injuries occurred six times more often in Canadian Peewee (12 to 13 years old) checking leagues compared to non-checking leagues. Players in this age group are at different levels of maturity with a wide variation in height, weight, and strength. These discrepancies may contribute to collision-induced injuries.

Puck velocities of 120 mph in professional players and 50 mph in peewee players have been documented. Puck impact on a face mask may result in deformation of the mask and face contact if the velocity exceeds 60 mph. Sticks remain a significant cause of injury, especially to the head and face; however, the incidence has decreased due to mandatory use of helmets with face masks in most leagues, along with more strict enforcement of high sticking penalties. The risk of head and facial injuries in Junior Hockey in the United States remains a concern due to the fact that players over the age of 18 years are not required to wear any facial protection. The most common injury reported in a 3 year prospective study of a United States Hockey League team was a facial laceration typically caused by an opposing players' stick in the 3rd period of a game.[46]

TYPES OF INJURY

Most injuries reported in the past occurred in the head and neck region. Since Minnesota first required helmets and full face masks for all players in 1975, permanent eye and dental injuries have decreased. An average of 272 eye injuries per year, including 32 cases of blindness, were documented among Canadian players before the use of face masks. The number of reported injuries decreased to 94 with the use of face protectors. No permanent eye injury has been documented in a player wearing a Canadian Standards Association certified mask. A prospective cohort observational analysis was performed in the United States Hockey League (USHL) during the 1997-8 regular season & playoffs (unpublished data).

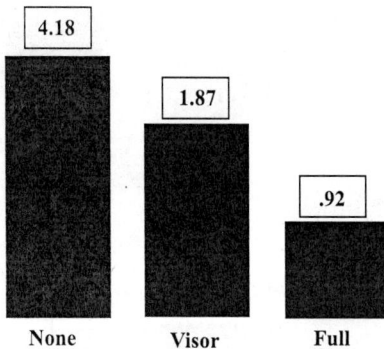

Bar chart: None 4.18, Visor 1.87, Full .92

[46] Stuart, M.J.; Smith, A.M.; Kaufman, M.: *Injuries in Junior A Ice Hockey: A Three-Year Prospective Study,* Am J Sports Med., 1995, 23(4) p. 458-461.

The number, type, location, and severity of head, facial, and neck injuries sustained during Junior A hockey games were recorded in order to examine the relationship between head/facial injuries with the type of facial protection (i.e., none, partial, full). The overall injury rate was over 4 times higher for players without facial protection, injury risk decreased with the use of a visor (half-shield), and was lowest for players with full facial protection (full cage or full shield). The risk of eye injury was greatest without facial protection (none = 0.17, visor = 0.02, full = 0 per player game) and no relationship was identified between the type of facial protection and the risk of concussion.

Neck (cervical spine) fractures and spinal cord injuries with paralysis occur in ice hockey. The most common mechanism involves a player hitting the boards with the top of his or her head and the neck in a slightly flexed (bent forward position). Prevention of these catastrophic injuries is essential. Players, coaches, and officials must ensure that dangerous tactics, such as checking from behind near the boards, are prohibited. Players must stay in control when giving a check and maintain a safe body position when accepting a check. It is important to always "keep your head up" to avoid a collision when the top of the head strikes the boards or another player. Sliding on the ice can be very dangerous and players should turn their body or use their shoulder, arms, or legs to strike the boards if a collision is inevitable.

Contusions (bruises) and lacerations (cuts) account for approximately 75 percent of hockey injuries. Ligament sprains, joint dislocations, and fractures are caused by contact. The shoulder is a frequent site of direct impact that may result in a shoulder separation (acromioclavicular joint or AC joint), a shoulder dislocation (glenohumeral joint), or a fracture of the clavicle (collarbone). Medial collateral ligament sprains (inside the knee) are caused by a blow to the outside of the knee. Non-contact injuries, such as hip flexor and groin muscle strains, result from the large forces generated during a quick skating start. Thumb ligament (ulnocollateral) tears can occur when the firmly gripped stick is pulled away, similar to the skier's thumb injury.

PREVENTION

The intrinsic hazards of playing hockey cannot be completely eliminated, but the risk of injury can be substantially decreased. Further study of ice hockey injuries by a comprehensive recording system is essential to identify factors that will allow prevention. Athletes spend a lot of time and effort developing their bodies. Knowledge about ways to safely train and compete along with an understanding about how to avoid and recover from injury will help players reach their goals. We completed a 2-year prospective evaluation of injuries in Junior A ice hockey which provided valuable insight. Injuries to Junior A hockey players expressed in 1000 player game hours were greater for Junior A players than for college and Swedish professionals. Many Junior A players do not wear facial protection. Because most of the injuries were to the head and face, lack of adequate protection was identified as a contributing factor.

Pre-season screening with a pre-participation examination may uncover deficiencies and evaluate an individual's limitations. It is important to identify past medical problems which may require immediate attention or may result in specific needs during the season. Current medications are listed along with any allergies or previous adverse reactions to certain types of medicine. All past injuries are outlined so that intervention can be prescribed when appropriate to prevent recurrence. Preventative measures include a specific rehabilitation program, alteration in skating or checking technique, bracing or taping of unstable joints (thumb, knee, shoulder), and special padding and equipment modifications. The physical examination may identify tight muscle-tendon units that would benefit from a careful, focused stretching program (hip flexors, groin). Specific strength training exercises may eliminate areas of weakness that may precipitate an injury and may remedy any muscle strength imbalance. Significant strength gain in certain muscle groups (e.g., the neck muscles) may even decrease the risk of serious injury.

Effective stretching decreases the risk of soft tissue injury (Chapter 14), proper conditioning avoids physiological overload such as 'burnout' and 'overuse' injuries (Chapter 15), and a well-balanced diet based on sound nutritional principles provides the fuel for training and competition (Chapter 16 and 17). Readers are strongly encouraged to read <u>Over Speed</u> by Jack Blatherwick, Ph.D., the most complete book written on physiological training for ice hockey, published by USA Hockey.[47]

Properly fitting, quality equipment is essential for all hockey players. The wide-spread use of helmets has played a very important role in the prevention of serious brain injuries. Contrary to some concern, there is no conclusive evidence that the weight of the helmet is responsible for neck injuries. The increased incidence of neck injuries in the past ten years has been attributed to factors such as bigger, faster, and more aggressive players, and a lack of enforcement of rules designed to eliminate dangerous tactics such as checking from behind. The value of full facial protection has already been substantiated by the dramatic decrease in eye injuries. Based on our research, it appears that **the half-shield or visor improves protection, but is not as reliable as a full cage or shield.** The visor is commonly worn in a 'tilted-up' position to improve visibility, which renders it ineffective in shielding the face and eyes. The half-shield visor may actually

---

[47] Blatherwick, Jack Dr. *Over Speed: Skill Training for Hockey.* (USA Hockey: Colorado Springs, CO, 1992.)

direct the stick toward the eye thereby increasing the risk of serious injury. In a study we reported a few years ago, players wearing half-shields from a Junior A team sustained a total of six facial lacerations, one broken nose, and a fractured tooth. Only two chin lacerations were treated in players wearing a full cage, which could have been prevented by the use of an appropriately sized mask with a chin cup.

The acromioclavicular joint sprain, or separated shoulder, is clearly one of the most common injuries suffered by hockey players. We have attempted to decrease the risk of this injury by 'beefing up' the hockey shoulder pads. One-fourth to one-inch thick open foam cell channels are attached to the undersurface of the shoulder pad and placed directly over the acromion (point of the shoulder) to decrease the force of impact.

Shin pads have improved dramatically since the days of taping magazines to the front of the legs. A thigh extension may protect the vulnerable area between the end of the pants and the top of the knee pad which is left exposed when the knee is bent. This additional protection may help prevent deep muscle bruises. Shin pads with an ankle extension tucked beneath the skate tongue can prevent the potentially serious 'boot top' laceration that can occur between the turned down tongue and the end of the shin pad.

Strict enforcement of the rules of the game is a very important aspect of injury prevention. Elimination of fighting, spearing, and checking from behind along with minimizing the occurrence of high sticking, tripping, and boarding would significantly decrease the incidence of serious injury. The contention that sticks would come down if no one wore helmets or facemasks may have some merit. However, the equipment was developed to meet the need of injury protection in the first place (even accidental injuries in hockey are common and often serious). Furthermore, since sport is a microcosm of society and society is becoming more, not less, violent, the assumption of a voluntary increase in fair play may be idealistic. Most hockey organizations require this equipment at most levels, so players must get used to the idea and play within the rules.

TREATMENT

Injuries are best dealt with by making a prompt, accurate diagnosis of the problem so that treatment can be started immediately. Players who ignore or try to 'wish away' injuries are not doing themselves any good. Athletes who have a fear of being forced out of competition because of admitting to an injury may actually prolong their recovery by delaying appropriate treatment and risking further damage. Hockey players may have to play through pain at times, but if they listen to their bodies and seek the appropriate care, discomfort and swelling can be reduced, healing is promoted, and further injuries are prevented.

The immediate care of soft tissue injuries like contusions (bruises), sprains (ligament stretching or tearing), and strains (muscle or tendon stretching or tearing) involves the <u>PRICE</u> approach.

<u>P</u>rotection:	Splint, cast, cane, crutches
<u>R</u>est:	Activity modification
<u>I</u>ce:	Cold therapy
<u>C</u>ompression:	Elastic bandage
<u>E</u>levation:	Above level of your heart

Frequently there is confusion about when to use ice or heat. Cryotherapy (cold) and thermotherapy (heat) both have a place in the treatment of soft tissue injuries. Contusions, sprains, and strains result in soft tissue damage and inflammation. Increased blood flow to the area of inflammation results in swelling, warmth, redness, and tenderness. Muscle spasm is the body's effort to splint the damaged tissue to prevent further injury. Pressure from the swelling and spasm causes more pain resulting in a vicious cycle (pain → spasm → pain, etc.).

Cold therapy decreases the tissue temperature and blood flow which consequently decreases swelling, inflammation, muscle spasm, bleeding, and pain.

Recommended Use of Cryotherapy

WHEN: Immediately after injury, repeat after showering, repeat several times each day until swelling and warmth have resolved. 20 to 30 minutes in duration progressing through the stages of cold, burning, aching and, finally, numbness.

HOW: Ice bag: Chipped or crushed ice conforms better than cubes.

Chemical cold pack: Expensive but convenient, cannot be reused, variable temperature and duration of cold.

Synthetic gel pack: Conforms well, stays below freezing for about 15 minutes, wrap in towel and do not place directly on skin (to prevent frostbite).

Ice cup: Strip back rim of paper cup to expose ice, massage area until numb and skin turns bright red. Cold slush: Mix ice chips in water, submerge limb wrapped in a wet elastic wrap.

Cold spray: Expensive but convenient, may cause skin reaction, does not penetrate deeply to control internal bleeding.

CAUTION: "More is not better"

Avoid use of ice in the presence of poor circulation or hypersensitivity to cold

Avoid prolonged application over superficial nerves (elbow).

Heat therapy increases the tissue temperature and blood flow which consequently decreases pain and muscle spasm while facilitating increased range of motion.
Recommended Use of Thermotherapy

WHEN: After acute inflammation subsides
            Swelling stabilized
            No redness
            Near full range of motion
            No pain with motion
            Progress when the use of ice plateaus

HOW: Hot pack: Wrap in several layers of towel to prevent burning.

Heating pad: Avoid lying on the pad because pressure from body weight can impede the circulation necessary to dissipate the accumulated heat.

Whirlpool: Water temperature of 98 to 106 degrees F for about 20 minutes. May cause dizziness and heat stress, athletes should never be unsupervised.

Analgesic balms: Apply to the skin and cover with a towel for insulation. These may irritate the skin.

CAUTION: Do not apply heat immediately after injury.
            Avoid use in the presence of poor sensation, poor circulation, hypersensitivity to heat, or fever.
Players who truly understand the game of hockey should also have a working knowledge about injury prevention

and treatment. There is no way to eliminate the risk of injury completely, but the number and severity of injuries can be significantly decreased by paying strict attention to conditioning, strengthening, stretching, properly fitting quality equipment, identification of training errors, prompt, accurate diagnosis followed by the appropriate treatment and strict enforcement of rules to eliminate the truly dangerous and unnecessary aspects of the game.

The following table is primarily based on research studies conducted by Stuart and Smith, which have all used the same injury diagnosis and the same level of health care provider making the diagnosis. The results are expressed in injuries per 1000 hours of player game hours so the results are comparable between studies.

Table 2.
Summary of Literature for Incidence of Injury in Practices and Games Stratified by Level of Participation

Injury rates / 1,000

Level	Ages Years	Practice	Game
Squirt	9 - 10	1.2	00.0
Peewee	11 - 12	2.5	00.0
Bantam	13 - 14	2.5	10.9
High School	15 - 19	.2	34.4
Jr. Varsity	15 - 18	.5	30.3
Varsity	16 - 19	0	49.7
Junior A	17 - 19	3.9	96.1
Intercollegiate	18 - 21	2.3	84.3
Swedish elite (1988)	19 - 33	1.4	78.4
Swedish elite (1993)	--------	2.6	74.1

Note: No game injuries occurred for Squirt or Peewee and no injuries occurred in practices for the varsity high school players.

Dr. Mike Stuart (left) and Dr. Gerald Malanga (center) complete a thorough physical examination, ruling out previous or present injuries or potential problems. Dr. Stuart is very involved on task forces and as a team physician with USA Hockey.

Dr. Hugh Smith, Chairman of Cardiovascular Diseases at Mayo Clinic helps out with screening physicals.

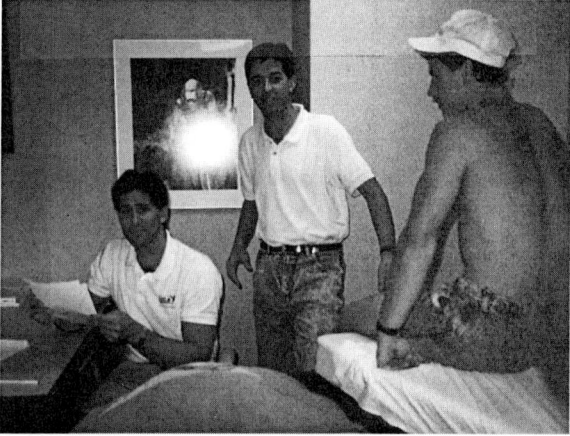

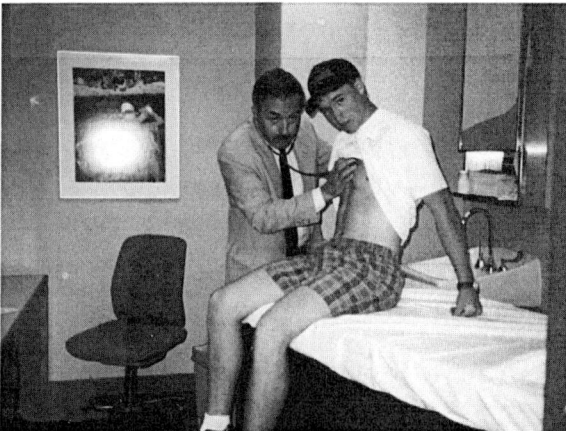

THE PSYCHOLOGICAL REHABILITATION OF ICE HOCKEY INJURIES

As noted from the discussion on the types of injuries sustained in ice hockey, it is evident that most are of a relatively minor nature. However, each season, several serious injuries occur, even at the junior hockey level, which may require that a player remain out of hockey for the season. This can be very depressing for hockey players whose dreams may be linked to college scholarships, national teams, or moving from a minor league franchise to the NHL. The fear of being replaced on the team is extremely threatening when one considers the hard work and discipline that earned the player a position on the team in the first place. No matter the level of participation, the consequences of injury are that players face a loss of control and see themselves as unable or unlikely to meet their season's goals. Early research on injured athletes showed a period of depression and anger in those who were seriously injured. These feelings gradually improved as the player recovered physically.[48] Subsequent studies by this author and her colleagues at Mayo Clinic have investigated the impact of injury on 13 sport teams, four of which were hockey teams, and the results show significant post-injury depression, anger, and decreased energy.

Players usually miss little or no playing time for most hockey injuries, but those who are forced to stop playing might benefit from seeing a sport counselor while they are receiving treatment from their physician, athletic trainer, or physical therapist. Seriously injured athletes may benefit from an opportunity to confidentially express the meaning of their injury and how it has impacted on their career dreams and season goals. If a player can express depression and anger in a non-threatening atmosphere, it frequently helps the athlete

---

[48] Smith, Aynsley. *The Emotional Responses of Athletes to Injury.*

to let go and move from "emotion-focused" to "problem-focused" coping strategies. Because most sport injuries that are serious require a significant investment by athletes in their rehabilitation, commitment and motivation are necessary for optimal recovery to occur.

Anger is more harmful than the injury that caused it

Injured hockey players should use the goal setting, relaxation, imagery, and responsibility-taking chapters in this book to help them progress through the rehabilitation period. For example, a goal setting 'target' is drawn where the substituted dream goal is to return to play at a similar or improved level. The next target ring may be for physician checks, often 3-4 weeks apart. The next ring might be athletic trainer or physical therapy appointments where it is important to measure flexion achieved and strength gains to document the rehabilitation process. The bull's-eye, or center of the target, usually consists of daily goals such as stretching, biking, weights, icing, etc. When the goals of the target model are appropriate to the player's condition and consistent with the goals of therapy, they serve as both a schedule and motivation for rehabilitation.

Rehabilitation of sports injuries usually run an up/down course and the 'mentally tough' athlete who sees adversity as a challenge and can remain goal directed usually has the most optimal recovery. One hockey player, Todd Huyber, who was on a full scholarship to an East coast college had many injuries occur at crucial times in his career. One year he stopped to see me, heavily bandaged from another injury which had recently required surgery. When I inquired what had happened he answered, "It was one more obstacle that the Great Hockey God put in my path to see me overcome." Consistent with his own attitude, he overcame the obstacles to play again. However, some severe injuries do not rehab

Consistent with his own attitude, he overcame the obstacles to play again. However, some severe injuries do not rehab well and an athlete may need assistance in accepting a less than ideal outcome.

POSITIVE COPING WITH HOCKEY INJURIES

Rehabilitation periods are ideal times to read books about hockey technique, sports nutrition, power skating, strength and conditioning, sport psychology, and mental toughness. By closely watching games and tapes of hockey, an injured athlete can use this time for learning experiences and role modeling opportunities. Handling one's stick, fooling with a tennis ball or puck, video games, and juggling are ways to keep eye-to-hand reactions fast and maintain a 'feel'. Depending upon the nature of the injury, aerobic conditioning to maintain strength and endurance should be attempted. During rehabilitation, weight-vests, aquacizers, and upper body exercise equipment are often prescribed by the physician, therapist, or athletic trainer. Maintaining conditioning enhances a positive mood state, increases confidence, and hastens the rehabilitation period by decreasing the loss and frustration which accompanies exercise restriction.

By too much sitting still, the body becomes unhealthy and soon the mind – Longfellow

16

STRETCHING AND WARM-UP PRINCIPLES FOR HOCKEY

Dave Krause, P.T.

INTRODUCTION

Flexibility is defined as the range of motion in a joint or series of joints. One method to increase flexibility is by stretching, which primarily targets the muscle(s). The goals of the warm-up and stretching exercises are to allow the athlete to work more efficiently at a higher level of performance and, hopefully, to prevent injury.

EFFECTS

Both psychological and physiological benefits may be achieved with stretching and a proper warm-up routine. Stretching and a warm-up period promote relaxation and provide a period of concentration as you prepare for practice or a game. Physiological benefits include:

- increases in heart rate, respiratory rate, and oxygen uptake
- elevation of the muscle temperature (allows for faster and more forceful contractions)
- lubrication of the joints via joint fluids
- increased agility (warmer temperatures in the muscle allows for greater elasticity)
- decreased muscle tension
- decreased residual muscle soreness
- increased flexibility (long term)

WHEN:

The exercises should begin 30-40 minutes before games and should taper off 10-15 minutes prior to the competition, which will allow for recovery from temporary fatigue without the loss of the warm-up benefits. Depending on the environment, the effects of the warm-up and stretching period can be expected to last approximately 30 minutes, thus time should be spent stretching and warming up prior to the start of the second and third periods.

Stretching and warm up exercises are not restricted to pre-game or pre-practice routine. The principles should be applied after prolonged breaks in practice and, as mentioned, prior to each period. In addition, players who have been 'getting cold' on the bench should stretch prior to entering the game.

TECHNIQUE

Ideally, the player should break into *a sweat* prior to stretching by skating around the rink, etc. After warming up, the player should perform *slow, prolonged* stretching. Bouncing will not produce an effective stretch! The player should ease into and out of the stretch. The stretch should be held a minimum of 20 seconds. Relaxation and concentration are essential. The player must remember to stretch within his own limits. It should not be painful nor should it be competitive. It is also not necessary when stretching to attempt to reach a maximum range of motion.

FREQUENT INJURIES

Two frequently injured regions in the hockey player are the groin and the hip flexors (front of the hip). Stretching of these two areas is essential. Any hockey player who has experienced a groin pull as a result of inadequate stretching knows the crippling effect this injury can have on his game, sometimes to the point of having to miss ice-time. Specific stretches for these and other muscles/regions may be found in various sources, such as *Stretching,* by Bob Anderson.[49]

---

[49] Anderson, Bob

17

STRENGTH TRAINING AND CONDITIONING FOR HOCKEY

John P. Tomberlin III

Ice Hockey is one of the most vigorous team sports and requires tremendous physical conditioning. Hockey demands a high level of continuous aerobic conditioning combined with intense bursts of anaerobic power and speed. Lower body strength is necessary for quick acceleration in skating and upper body strength is vital for puck handling, shooting, and checking. These attributes are essential for playing hockey at a high level of skill and competition, as well as for injury prevention.

Specificity of training is a key to training for any sport, and ice hockey is no exception. A conditioning program must be done predominantly on the ice. This conditioning should include both continuous aerobic activity and the anaerobic bursts so vital to hockey. Dry-land training is a good supplement to off-season training and especially useful when ice time is limited. Conditioning exercises should be hockey-specific and dry-land training such as sprints and leg strengthening should only be used in the off-season and pre-season. Sliding boards and roller blades can be useful when ice time is not available, but there is no substitute for skating!

Periodization is the key to the hockey players' strength training program. The periodization-approach provides cyclic changes in intensity (workload) and volume (total sets and repetitions) to keep muscles stimulated and ready to respond to variations in stress. The 'cycling' of workouts helps prevent the common plateauing and 'staleness' most training regimens seem to cause.

The following table and exercises are to be used

as guidelines in conjunction with your coaches' preferred routine.

Purpose*	Size	Strength	Power	Performance**
Intensity	Low	High	High	High -- Low
Repetitions	12 - 20	6 - 12	3 - 6	6 -- 12
Sets	3 - 5	3 - 5	3 - 5	2 -- 3
Workouts***	4/wk	4/wk	4/wk	2/wk

*   The purpose of this approach is to cycle 1-3/year, 2-3 months per cycle, from the "size to strength to power" training. Each component (size, strength, and power) would be approximately 4 weeks in length to accommodate a 12 week (3 month) cycle.

** The performance phase should be timed to occur from mid-season to playoffs. During tournaments and playoffs, it may be advisable to discontinue strength training to prevent burnout. Tapering the workouts toward the end of the season is recommended.

*** 4/wk means that two different exercise routines are being performed 2 times a week.
Example: Two times per week— Monday and Wednesday
Strength Training Exercise Options *#
1. Size/ Strength/ Power Phases**
Chest: Bench Press, Flys, "Pec"- Deck
A.
2/wk   Shoulders: Military Press, Bar Dips, Upright Rowing

Arms: Bicep and Tricep Curls

B.

2/wk   Legs: Traditional or hack squat, leg press, quad extension, hamstring curls

Back: Pull-ups, seated chest row, lat pulldowns, situps

Wrist: Wrist curl, wrist extensions, slap-shot, and reverse slap-shot motion

* A weight belt is highly recommended for all strength training exercises. It is not usually advisable to workout alone - use a partner.

Warm-up and stretching before, and cool down and stretching after workouts, is strongly advised. Rest between sets should be at least 1-3 minutes.

** During the performance phase, it is recommended to workout 2/wk; therefore on one day, the A routine would be done, and on the other day, the B routine would be done.

SUMMARY

Off-Season:

The goal here is to *build* for the future, not just to maintain. Conditioning should be done preferably on the ice and off-ice strength training builds hypertrophy (muscle size) and strength. Repetitive skill training should be integrated to bridge the gap between training for hockey and playing hockey.

Pre-Season:

The goal here is to maximize the gains in strength and conditioning from off-season training as soon as possible.

Performing position-specific drills and integrating situation play and strategy are a very important part of the season's preparation.

In-Season:

Game play, strategy, and position-specific skills should receive priority at this time. Mid-season burnout can easily be prevented by variations in the strength and conditioning program. The key here is to train to maintain, but skate to win.

18

NUTRITION TIPS FOR THE HOCKEY PLAYER

Steve DeBoer, M.P.H., R.D., L.D. and Kathy Krause, R.D.

Proper nutrition forms the foundation for physical performance. All food can serve as fuel for energy but no one food can provide all the essential nutrients. Instead, athletes need a balance of carbohydrates, protein, and fat, plus vitamins, minerals, and water.

Ice hockey is unique because it demands well developed aerobic and anaerobic energy systems. The hockey player focuses on the improvement of both aerobic and anaerobic endurance, muscular strength, skating speed, and specific hockey skills. By carefully selecting foods and beverages, the athlete can obtain the ideal balance of necessary nutrients.

CALORIES

It has been estimated that calorie needs for hockey players range from 4,000 to more than 6,000 calories per day. Most of this energy is needed for playing and training, while some of the calories are required for the resting body and ordinary daily activities.

CARBOHYDRATES

The main function of carbohydrate is to serve as energy fuel for the body in both aerobic and anaerobic exercise. Complex carbohydrates (complex CHO) should provide more than half of the day's calories. Examples of complex carbohydrates are bread, pasta, cereal, rice, potatoes, beans, and vegetables. Simple carbohydrates such as table sugar, jam, jelly, candy, and cookies should be limited. These foods can supply energy but contain few vitamins and minerals. They may also weaken athletic performance if taken shortly before a game or an event, in those individuals more prone to hypoglycemia. Some athletes do not experience this low blood sugar effect, but this should be determined during practice sessions, not prior to a game.

PROTEIN

More than enough protein is obtained when the daily diet includes a minimum of 15% of the calories in the form of protein. Protein provides only about 5% of the fuel during exercise. Most protein is used for the building and repair of muscles and other body tissues. The typical American diet contains 50-100% more protein than required. Protein supplements, powders, or tablets are unnecessary unless the hockey player has difficulty eating adequate calories. Enough protein will be supplied in the diet if at least 6-8 ounces of meat/meat substitutes (lean beef, chicken, fish, eggs, or an equivalent amount of dried beans, peas, or peanut butter) and 3 servings of low-fat dairy products (1% milk, low-fat cheese, or yogurt) are eaten daily.

FATS

The diet should provide 20-30% of the total daily calories from fat. Examples of foods that provide fat in the diet include fried foods (including chips and donuts), margarine, full-fat dairy products (butter, whole milk, cheese, ice cream), baked goods (cookies, biscuits, pastries, muffins, cake, pie), candy bars, oils, nuts, seeds, salad dressing, and gravy. These foods should be limited so the hockey player has room to eat enough energy efficient carbohydrates. Eating lean meats and low-fat dairy products helps limit saturated fat in the diet, which can contribute to the development of heart disease.

VITAMINS/MINERALS

By eating a well-balanced diet with a variety of foods from each food group in the Food Guide Pyramid (see page 171), the athlete eliminates the need for vitamin/mineral supplementation. A well-balanced diet will provide these nutrients. Since the hockey player needs more food than the non-athlete, more vitamins and minerals are consumed, if foods in the Fats and Sweets group are eaten in moderation. Vitamin or mineral supplementation is only beneficial if one has a known deficiency, such as iron supplementation for someone with iron-deficiency anemia.

FLUIDS

Adequate fluid intake is vital to the athlete. Proper hydration is the most frequently overlooked aid to athletic performance. A water loss of as little as 2% of body weight can reduce hockey effectiveness.

Fluid requirements:

20 ounces (2 1/2 glasses) - 1-2 hours before exercise.

5-10 ounces (1 ounce = approx. 1 gulp) every 15-20 minutes during exercise.

To help rehydrate the body after exercise, a good rule of thumb is to drink 24 ounces (3 glasses) of fluid for every 1 pound of weight loss.

FLUID TYPE

The hockey player should drink plenty of water since the body itself consists of 60% water. Sport drinks such as Gatorade and Powerade may be beneficial if exercise lasts more than 1 hour. These drinks may help the athlete exercise longer before reaching exhaustion by helping to maintain blood sugar levels. Fruit juices and soda pop have too high a concentration of sugar to be absorbed very quickly, unless they are diluted to 50% strength.

ERGOGENIC SUPPLEMENTS

There are many supplements available that claim to be performance-enhancing, or ergogenic. Good research studies usually show that they provide no benefit to athletes, though they will reduce funds in their bank accounts. In addition, some of these supplements can be harmful to health. The most performance-enhancing substances actually turn out to be water, carbohydrate, and the other nutrients the body requires.

Among those supplements that have been adequately tested, the only one that might prove helpful to the hockey player is creatine. It has been shown to cause weight gain, some of which may be muscle. Several studies have shown that athletes who use creatine perform better in some laboratory tests of strength. However, some laboratory tests have not shown improved performance with use of creatine, and performance in regular sporting events has not been tested enough. Side effects include diarrhea, muscle cramping, and muscle tears. Long term side effects past 6-8 weeks have not been studied. Safety in high school athletes has not been studied at all. The hockey player considering use of creatine or other supplements is advised to discuss the supplement with a physician or dietitian knowledgeable in sports medicine and nutrition first.

WEIGHT LOSS

The hockey player should try to achieve, and then maintain, an appropriate body weight as well as optimal body composition. The most important factor to any weight loss diet is safety. The diet needs to be nutritious and adequate in all major food groups with a sufficient amount of calories. Since the goal of weight loss is to lose body fat, the weight loss should be slow to prevent muscle breakdown. Weight loss is best accomplished by a combination of aerobic exercise and decreasing food intake by no more than 500 calories per day, preferably prior to the start of the sport season.

WEIGHT GAIN

The only way to gain muscle tissue is to do muscle work, which means strength building exercises. It is preferable to accomplish this also during the off season. It is important to combine these exercises with an increased amount of calories. These extra calories should come mainly from carbohydrates, the body's preferred source of energy. Consuming extra calories without doing extra strength building exercises will typically increase weight mainly in the form of body fat. Liquid meals such as Carnation Instant Breakfast and Ensure may be used to increase caloric intake since they are easily digestible, high in carbohydrates, and provide fluid.

PRE-GAME NUTRITION

Foods should pass through the stomach and upper small intestine before an event. Meals should be eaten three to four hours before a game. A low fat meal is recommended because fats can take as long as five hours to leave the stomach, carbohydrates about two hours, and proteins approximately three hours. Foods that irritate the stomach by producing stool bulk or cause gas should be avoided.

<u>An Example of n 1100 Calorie Pre-Event Meal</u>

(61% carbohydrate, 19% fat, 20% protein)
12 oz. 1 % milk
2 cups cooked pasta
1 tsp olive oil
2 oz ground beef meatballs
2 Tbsp grated Parmesan cheese
1- 1 /2 cups spaghetti sauce
4 graham crackers
12 oz. fruit juice or 2 large fruits.

For those hockey players who experience no side effects when eating closer to exercise, a smaller snack of 350-500 calories could be eaten two hours before the game or practice.

POST-GAME NUTRITION

After an event or vigorous practice, the hockey player's body again needs a high carbohydrate diet to replenish fuel stores or performance may be affected at the next workout. The carbohydrate is stored more efficiently in the first few hours after exercise, so if one doesn't feel like eating, consuming a beverage high in carbohydrate is recommended. Fruit juice is one good example. Some sports drinks are made higher in carbohydrate for this purpose as well.

An Example of a One Day 4500 Calorie Meal Plan

(53% carbohydrate, 30% fat, 17% protein)

Breakfast
1-1 /2 cups dry cereal
3 toaster waffles or 3 slices toast
2 tsp margarine
8 oz orange juice
2 tsp peanut butter
2-4 Tbsp syrup
12 oz. 1 % milk

A.M. Snack
1 large apple

Noon
2 sandwiches made from:
4 slices bread
4 slices lunch meat
2 tsp mayonnaise or margarine
lettuce and tomato
1 cup of soup or 1/2 cup potato
salad
10-12 vanilla wafers or
gingersnaps
12 oz. 1% milk

Afternoon Snack
1 oz low-fat cheese
2 slices bread
12 oz juice

Dinner
5 oz. chicken, beef, fish
2 cups rice, pasta, or potato
1 cup corn or peas
salad or cooked vegetable
2 tsp margarine or 2 Tbsp
salad dressing
12 oz. 1 % milk

P.M. Snack
2 cups low-fat ice cream
4 Tbsp chocolate topping
1 banana
1 small handful nuts

Eat To Compete!

Food Guide Pyramid

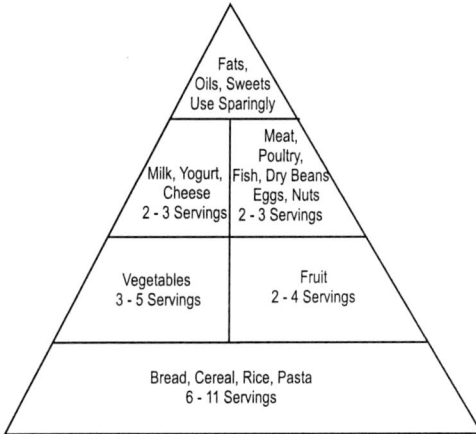

Fats,
Oils, Sweets
Use Sparingly

Milk, Yogurt,
Cheese
2 - 3 Servings

Meat,
Poultry,
Fish, Dry Beans
Eggs, Nuts
2 - 3 Servings

Vegetables
3 - 5 Servings

Fruit
2 - 4 Servings

Bread, Cereal, Rice, Pasta
6 - 11 Servings

19

TEAM TRAVEL

Hockey teams frequently travel internationally so that players of all ages can compete and gain experience in World Tournaments, the Olympics, and in exhibition games. The ability of hockey players, coaches, and support staff to adapt readily to new and changing conditions is important and can increase the team's likelihood of success. The advantage or edge one team might enjoy may be related to the team's ability to adapt quickly to time zone changes and a different environment. The challenge of coping with changes due to transit and the effect these changes have on athletic performance have been reported.[50]

Based on a review of the literature and practical experience, the following suggestions are made:

1. As soon as players board the plane, watches should be set to the new time zone of the destination city.

2. Players should try to eat and sleep on the schedule of the city of their destination.

3. If players are traveling from west to east, they should be advised to sleep very little while traveling and then sleep 8-10 hours when they go to bed, at the appropriate time on their new schedule. When traveling from east to west, it is the opposite and sleeping while on the plane is encouraged.

4. Avoid dehydration. Air travel is very 'drying' and hockey players are encouraged to carry a bottle of water with

---

[50] Davis, James O. "Strategies for Managing Athletes' Jet Lag".

them. Because they use up so much fluid skating in games and practices, it is important that hockey players not further dehydrate during travel. For the World Junior Championships in 1991, the players were asked to fill their water bottles in the airport in Boston and have an empty water bottle when they landed. They were asked to be responsible for traveling with a full bottle of water at all times while in Europe.

5. Hockey players should avoid caffeine, chocolate, and alcohol because these have a diuretic effect and void fluids from the body. In addition, these substances may provide unnecessary stimulation or insomnia.

6. Junk food should be avoided. Jim Johannson, a player on two U.S. Olympic Team who was a veteran of many international competitions, suggested that all junk food be avoided.

7. Ideally, practices should be scheduled soon after arrival in the foreign country. This promotes a feeling of familiarity and provides the player with a post-travel workout and relaxation period.

8. It is important that the team adapt readily, thus assuming and expecting success.

To facilitate adaptation to travel in a foreign country, hockey players are asked to anticipate things that will be different for them and plan ahead to ease their adjustment. For example, although the food in Germany is different, athletes can easily find the right percentage of complex carbohydrates, proteins, and fats recommended. Information on eating on the run was provided to each player prior to their participation at the World Junior Tournament in Zurich and the same information is included here for you.[51]

TIPS FOR THE TRAVELING ATHLETE

Nancy Clark, M.S., R.D. feels that athletes who travel have an added challenge; they need to find adequate carbohydrate-rich meals/snacks in restaurants, delis, and fast-foods. Although, many athletes at home are faithful to their high carbohydrate sports-diet during training and before competitions, too frequently when traveling, they dine on whatever happens to be easiest at that moment. Too often, this diet is too high in fat (donuts, hamburgers, french fries, chips, etc.). Although you may be tempted to persuade yourself that you deserve this break from your routine because you are tired, hungry, stressed, anxious, lonely, bored, or a combination of these, you may also be compromising your performance.

The occasional high fat meal will not interfere with top training, but a steady, fast-food diet will. To accommodate a high carbohydrate sports diet into your traveling routine, it is important to make the effort to eat a hearty, high carbohydrate breakfast. This prevents you from getting too hungry where you might be less likely to care about what you eat.

BREAKFAST

1. At a restaurant, when possible, order pancakes, french toast, whole wheat toast, bagels, bran, or corn muffins. Add jelly, jam, or syrup for extra carbohydrates but 'hold the butter' or request that it be served on the side.

2. Order a large orange juice for vitamin C and potassium. This order can compensate for a lack of fruits or vegetables in other meals.

---

[51] Clark, Nancy. R.D., M.S.

3. Clark suggests that in a hotel, you can save time and money by packing along your own cereal, raisins, and spoon. Either bring powdered milk or buy a half-pint of lowfat milk the night before at a convenience store, refrigerating it in ice from the hotel's ice machine.

LUNCH

1. Find a deli/restaurant that offers wholesome breads and request a sandwich that emphasizes the bread, rather than the filling. Pass on the mayonnaise and instead use mustard or ketchup, sliced tomatoes, and lettuce as condiments. Add more carbohydrates along with yogurt for dessert, juices, and fruits.

2. Hamburgers, fried fish, and french fries, available at fast-food restaurants have a very high fat content. Clarke suggests sticking to the baked potato, chili, thick-crust pizza, or salad bar. Request extra bread or rolls.

3. At the salad bar, generously pile on the chick peas, three-bean salad, toasted croutons. Take lots of bread but go easy on salad dressings and avoid mayonnaise-smothered pasta and potato salads.

4. Baked potatoes are a super choice if you request them plain. Avoid drenching them with butter, sour cream, and cheese. Wendy's cheese-stuffed potato, for example, offers 52% of the calories from fat (the equivalent of 9 teaspoons of butter). For moistness, try mashing the potato with milk rather than butter.

5. Hearty soups, such as split pea, minestrone, lentil, vegetable, and noodle accompanied by crackers, bread,

plain bagel, English muffin, or corn muffin provide a satisfying carbohydrate-rich, lowfat meal.

6. Although soft drinks are carbohydrate-rich, fruit juices are preferable sources of carbohydrates, vitamin C, and potassium.

DINNER

1. Visit restaurants that offer wholesome carbohydrates such as pasta, baked potatoes, rice, steamed vegetables, salad bars, homemade breads, fruit, juice, broiled foods, and other lowfat options.

2. Request thick-crust pizza with vegetable toppings rather than thin crust pizza with pepperoni or sausage.

3. Enjoy the bread/rolls either plain or with jelly. Replace the butter calories with another slice of bread, a second potato, soup and crackers, juice, or sherbet; all carbohydrate-rich choices.

4. When ordering salads, always request the dressing be served 'on the side'. Otherwise, you can get as many as 400 calories of oil/mayonnaise - fatty foods that fill your stomach but leave your muscles unfueled.

SNACKS AND MUNCHIES

1. Pack your own goodie grab bag. Some suggestions include: whole-grain bagels, muffins, rolls, crackers, pretzels, fig newtons, oatmeal raisin cookies, granola, raisins, and dried or fresh fruit.

2. Buy wholesome snacks at the convenience store - small packets of trail mix, raisins or dried fruit, yogurt, V-8 juice or fruit juice, a hot pretzel, slice of pizza or even a small sandwich, cup of soup, or hot cocoa.

Some emphasis during the four sessions with the Junior National Hockey Team prior to the World Tournament in 1991 was placed on concentrating on factors which were under the players' control. Focusing on only the aspects of travel that you have the ability and effort to influence is important. Therefore, wise food choices, keeping water bottles full, learning to concentrate on getting the rest you need, relaxation, reading, mental rehearsal, and a positive attitude are essential.

Delays, aviation difficulties, scheduling problems, or lack of ice for practice are all situations that may occur but situations over which the traveling athlete has little control. These are not major obstacles and need not get in the way of the team's success. By working on strategies geared toward enhancing team cohesion and stressing the importance of positive leadership, support, and caring, a team may hasten and help each other though the adaptation process, thereby promoting team success in international competitions.

20

WHAT IT MEANS TO BE A HOCKEY PLAYER

Steven B. Finnie, M.Ed. and Tracy L. Fischer, B.A.

"This is a great game, but it's a hard game." - Gretzky

Playing sports offers you an opportunity for success, improving skills, having fun, playing with friends, and achieving and maintaining fitness.[52] Most athletes begin playing competitive hockey while in grade school. Competing in sports at this young age instills self-confidence and pride, while encouraging cooperation, goal setting, and achievement. Winning, status, and external desires such as playing in a state tournament, being awarded a scholarship, or getting drafted become a priority to some players as they mature.

Your involvement and success in hockey, which is often reinforced by your family and friends, can prompt you to identify yourself as an "athlete," or as a "hockey player." This is called an "athletic identity" (A.I.). "Athletic identity" consists of thoughts, feelings, behaviors, and social effects integral to the individual who identifies with the athletic role.[53] To what extent does hockey play a role in your life or in your athletic identity'?

Exercise 1

In the circle below, draw the pieces of "pie" that represent what you consider to be your most important roles in your

[52] Gould, D. and Horn, T.S. Participation motivation in young athletes. In J.M. Silva & R.S. Weinberg (Eds.), (Human Kinetics:Champaign, IL. 1984), pp. 359-370.
[53] Brewer, B.W., Van Raalte, J.L. and Linder, D.E. Athletic Identity: Hercules' Muscles or Achilles' Heel? 1993;237-254.

life right now (e.g., student, employee, hockey player, family member, friend, etc.). Draw the pieces in relation to the size or importance of the roles you play, while drawing as many pieces of pie as necessary.

How big is the piece that represents your role as a hockey player (if you drew it in at all)? This will give you a good idea of how strong your athletic identity is.

Does it matter whether you call yourself a student, hockey player, or something else? Pursuing a career in hockey involves years of commitment. Although playing to the best of your ability and reaping the rewards of your investment will benefit you long after you stop playing hockey, some athletes may be overly invested in hockey. It is unhealthy when players depend on nothing but hockey for self-validation and neglect other aspects of their lives.[54] When an athlete's focus is solely on hockey (too strong an athletic identity), education and social goals become secondary to their athletic achievement.[55]

During high school and college, the focus on hockey and the expectations of an NHL career may result in a failure to develop career alternatives. Although only one in five hockey players receive college scholarships and 1% of those play professionally, surprisingly few players consider life after hockey. For example, many athletes are forced to leave hockey due to an injury and most are unprepared for this unexpected role change. Players may find this sudden role-reversal out of hockey difficult and without another role in life to play,

---

[54] Taylor, J. and Ogilvie, B.C. A conceptual model of adaptation to retirement among athletes. 1994; 1-20.
[55] Baillie, P.H. Understanding retirement from sports: Therapeutic ideas for helping athletes in transition.

the huge transition is difficult.[56] Individuals with a strong A.I. are also highly susceptible to emotional and social adjustment difficulties upon leaving hockey unfulfilled.

You may not realize how strong you identify with your role as a hockey player. Athletes become increasingly focused as they progress in their sport. What happens when you overly identify with hockey and neglect addressing your roles as a student, family member, partner, or employee? What do you know about life outside of hockey'? Completing and scoring the Hockey Athletic Identity Measurement Scale (HAIMS, Exercise 2) will give you an idea of your hockey-athletic identity.

Exercise 2

The Hockey Athletic Identity Measurement Scale (HAIMS)
The HAIMS is a useful tool for measuring your identity as a hockey player. Complete it by marking an "X" in the space that best reflects the extent to which each statement relates to you. The example scale below will help you score your responses.

Example:

Strongly   Strongly
Agree   ____:____:____:____:____:____:____   Disagree
           7   6   5   4   3   2   1

I consider myself a hockey player.

Strongly   Strongly
Agree   ____:____:____:____:____:____:____   Disagree
           7   6   5   4   3   2   1
My goals are related to hockey.

---

[56] Baillie, P.H. Ibid.

Strongly
Agree ____:____:____:____:____:____:____ Strongly
Disagree
      7   6   5   4   3   2   1

Most of my friends are hockey players.

Strongly
Agree ____:____:____:____:____:____:____ Strongly
Disagree
      7   6   5   4   3   2   1

Hockey is the most important part of my life.

Strongly
Agree ____:____:____:____:____:____:____ Strongly
Disagree
      7   6   5   4   3   2   1

I spend more time thinking about hockey than anything else.

Strongly
Agree ____:____:____:____:____:____:____ Strongly
Disagree
      7   6   5   4   3   2   1

I need to participate in hockey to feel good about myself.

Strongly
Agree ____:____:____:____:____:____:____ Strongly
Disagree
      7   6   5   4   3   2   1

Other people see me mainly as a hockey player.

Strongly
Agree ____:____:____:____:____:____:____ Strongly
Disagree
      7   6   5   4   3   2   1

I feel bad about myself when I do poorly in hockey.

Strongly
Agree ____:____:____:____:____:____:____ Strongly
Disagree
      7   6   5   4   3   2   1

Hockey is the only important thing in my life.

Strongly
Agree   ____:____:____:____:____:____:____   Strongly
Disagree

       7   6   5   4   3   2   1

I would be very depressed if I were injured and could not compete in hockey.

Strongly
Agree   ____:____:____:____:____:____:____   Strongly
Disagree

       7   6   5   4   3   2   1

To score the HAIMS, sum the scores of the ten items. The scores for each item range from 1 (strongly disagree) to 7 (strongly agree). Therefore, the higher your total score, the higher your athletic identity is.

SCORE	IDENTITY
50-70	High, exclusive
31-49	Moderate
7-30	Low

Hockey players with a strong HAIMS score may define their self-worth by their participation and accomplishments and will be influenced by wins and losses. A positive self-concept may not continue past the limits of hockey. Essentially, when players have no other skills or activities that satisfy their ego the way hockey can, they may continue to define themselves by their status as a hockey player even after their playing days are over. Likewise, players who socialize solely within hockey may be "role restricted". Because these players are only able to interact with others within their sport,[57] their ability to take on other roles "after hockey" is limited.

---

[57] Taylor, J. and Ogilvie, B.C. A conceptual model of adaptation to retirement among athletes. 1994; 1-20.

ROLE CONFLICTS: PROBLEMS BALANCING HOCKEY WITH EVERYDAY LIFE

Conflict often results from trying to balance too many roles. Notably, student-athletes have difficulties with time management, study skills, limited peer relationships outside of sport, lack of career and social development opportunities, and a restricted self-concept or basis for self-worth. When one college team was asked to prioritize their stress, time management was the biggest problem. Such difficulties occur because of the demanding athletic and student roles (practices, games, travel, workouts, meetings, ete.).[58] Granted, it can be difficult to balance so many roles, but it can be done if you accept all of your responsibilities and just get the job done. A great example of balance is former University of Minnesota center, Brian Bonin, who graduated with a chemistry degree from the university's Institute of Technology Honors Program, was a two-time WCHA scoring champion, and 1996 Hobey Baker award winner.[59]

"We talked about a lot of things, mostly non-hockey things, and it was refreshing to see that (Bonin) wasn't one-dimensional." (Wong, p. 8C)

Hockey is an exciting sport and for most of you it will always be a significant part of your life, whether it is as a spectator, fan, coach, or player. Many dream of pursuing a professional hockey career, and for a fortunate minority this will come true. However, for the majority, it will simply be a stage of life that you devote much time and effort before moving onto college, a career, or a family. Therefore, balancing all of your roles as equally as possible will leave you better prepared for any unexpected changes that may occur.

---

[58] Chartrand, J.M. and Lent, R.W. Sports counseling: Enhancing the development of the student-athlete.
[59] Wong, G. A hobey kind of guy. March

21

LEARNING LIFE SKILLS THROUGH HOCKEY

Steven B. Finnie, M.Ed. and Tracy L. Fischer, B.A.

LIFE SKILLS

Hockey participation teaches valuable "life skills" applicable to all aspects of your life. Hockey provides the opportunity to view yourself as a talented athlete **and** as a talented individual. Via hockey, you can learn about yourself and others, while creating opportunities for yourself both inside and outside of hockey. However, if hockey completely dominates your life, you will miss out on those learning experiences, which will leave you unprepared for life's challenges.[60] Athletes with a strong athletic identity may lack life skills needed to cope with an injury or their exit from hockey. It is important to develop life skills and have a life separate from hockey.

Exercise 1

Identifying Life Skills
Without reading the paragraph below, list life skills you learned in hockey that can be used outside of sport (e.g., in a job interview or at school).

_____	_____
_____	_____
_____	_____
_____	_____
_____	_____
_____	_____

---

[60] Petitpas, et al.

Which characteristics are important to you, to your coach, and to your teammates? Which skills were learned in competition and which skills have held you in hockey? Which characteristics are employers and college admissions officers looking for? If these skills apply to different situations, then you possess life skills! Below are a few more possibilities[61]

organization	performance under pressure
teamwork	respect
meeting challenges	pushing yourself to the limit
communication	self-control
accepting criticism	self-motivation
goal setting	handling success/failure

TRANSFERRING THE SKILLS

Dave Shand, former defenseman for Toronto and Washington, returned to school to study law after he had finished his playing career. While in school, he was able to apply the skills he learned through playing hockey. "It was a challenge....1 don't think I had written anything besides Christmas cards for thirteen years." He'd been a good student, enjoyed law school, and felt his hockey experience helped him (the discipline, drive, and being goal orientated).[62] After a career-ending back surgery, Brian Engbloom discussed his rehabilitation and his plan for the future. He tried several jobs before becoming a commentator for ESPN. "Many people in the working environment don't know how to work together," Brian said, "Because of hockey, I learned about teamwork when I was nine. For these people it's a new concept."[63] Viewers watching the 1999 Stanley Cup playoffs enjoyed Brian's astute observations.

---

[61] Danish, Petitpas, and Halle
[62] McFalone, B.
[63] McFalone, Ibid.

Exercise 2

Now that you have read a few examples and listed your life skills, please answer the following questions[64]

1. How are your skills similar to those that employers are looking for? How might they be important for your future career development?

_____

_____

_____

_____

2. How will you apply lessons from hockey to life outside of hockey? How can these skills be important in life decisions you make?

_____

_____

_____

_____

3. Which life skills must you build and/or work on?

_____

_____

_____

_____

SPORT PSYCHOLOGY SKILLS

In addition to the skills discussed in this chapter, most skills discussed in Power Play as "mental toughness skills for hockey" apply to other areas of your life. For example, cognitive restructuring, mental imagery, goal setting, and

---

[64] Petitpas, et al.

motivation can be helpful in post-athletic careers. The results of one study showed that almost 90% of athletes who use sport psychology skills also use them for their new activities, interests, or careers after leaving sport.[65] Helpful was their experience in such things as setting goals, preparation plans, or imaging a successful performance. About 40% of study participants indicated they spent 4-6 hours per week doing some mental preparation. Those athletes exposed to mental training programs during their hockey careers have an advantage because the same skills apply to life.

EXIT FROM HOCKEY

Exiting from competitive hockey happens to all players, including "The Great One." Although Gretzky retired at the age of 38, this transition occurs for most players between high school and college. Athletes may **choose** to leave hockey (e.g., nagging injuries, age, declining performance, etc.) or are **forced** to quit (e.g., "cut" from the team, career-ending injury). Players may choose to quit because they have achieved their goals, they want to concentrate on a new career, or they may want to finish their career "on top" of the game.[66]

COMMON FEELINGS UPON EXIT FROM HOCKEY

Retired athletes may experience loss of confidence, identity, status, or anxiety about the future upon leaving hockey. Along with physiological changes (e.g., decreased metabolism, weight gain), they may feel isolation, regret, and depression. Teammates are important to hockey players and it is difficult to lose that social support. Consequently, athletes may grieve or feel lonely after their playing days have ended. Some athletes may welcome time away from hockey, realizing

---

[65] Koukouris
[66] Petitpas, et al.

it is an opportunity for personal growth. All these feelings are normal and will take time to work through.

THE TRANSITION PROCESS

A hockey career is shorter than most careers (few players continue hockey beyond 30). If you are prepared and have achieved your goals, the transition out of hockey may be a relief. If you are not prepared (lack support, skills, or preparation), it can be a shock. It is also possible, no matter what the circumstances, to feel both.

It takes an average of two years to adjust to life after hockey, although some struggle for years and others never adjust. The transition should be viewed as a process rather than as a traumatic event. It is helpful if you have other activities or interests (e.g., continuing your education, finding a new job) to occupy your time after hockey. Players like Ken Dryden who go on to write or practice law, or others like Larry Robinson, Lindy Ruff, and Barry Melrose who go on to coach or to provide a color commentary will find the transition process less traumatic as they are challenged by new responsibilities.

Long-term personal and social development is more important than short-term athletic success.
- Taylor and Ogilvie, P.

PLANNING FOR LIFE AFTER HOCKEY

Although a departure from competitive hockey is inevitable, most athletes are not mentally ready to discuss issues surrounding their exit from hockey while still actively competing. Nevertheless, it's not easy when the choice is suddenly taken from the player. For example, Gerry Desjardins, after getting a puck in the eye resulting in the premature end of his career, said, "It's not an easy thing to adjust to (retirement)...Hockey is your whole life. That's all you live for and all of a sudden it's no longer there. Business or no business ...it's quite an adjustment to make."[67]

Life after hockey requires life and financial planning, self-reliance, coping resources, goal assessment, education, career exploration, and creating opportunities. Planning is a good way to help athletes anticipate and adjust to the transition out of hockey. Clark Gillies (forward for the Islanders and Sabres) noted leaving hockey is "...not a fun thing to deal with. You can ask anybody who has played a professional sport or anybody that's done anything for as long as I played hockey. All of a sudden I had to try and figure out what to do with the rest of my life. I really had no idea what to do. So it was a tough transition."[68] By planning for the future now, you can make your eventual transition out of hockey an easier one. One player who worked with Aynsley knew he wanted to coach after his playing days were over. He studied the game and the coaching strategies of all coaches he played for determining what was and what wasn't effective. All the years he played professional hockey he was also preparing himself for his transition from player to coach. The following sections help you begin to prepare for life off the ice.

SELF-EXPLORATION

Know yourself, your interests, and values before you try to determine what career is best suited to you.[69] In addition to the life skills you identified in earlier in this chapter, to write a resume or succeed in a job interview, you must know the skills you possess and those you need to develop. If your job does not interest you, or you do not find value in it, you

---

[67] McFalone, ibid.
[68] McFalone, Ibid., p. 104
[69] Petitpas, et al.

will not enjoy it or stick with it. In sum, values are what are important to you, interests are what you enjoy doing, and skills are what you are good at.[70]

Exercise 3

Values, Interests, and Skills

Take a minute to list some of the values, interests, and skills that you have in hockey. Then complete Exercise 4 on personal values. These values, interests, and skills are likely to be the same ones that you will look for in other activities and pursuits outside of hockey.

Values (important)	Interests (enjoy)	Skills (good at)
_____	_____	_____
_____	_____	_____
_____	_____	_____
_____	_____	_____

Exercise 4

Personal Values Exercise

Rank the items by assigning the number 1 to the item that most describes you, working down to number 12 that which least describes you. Check the key at the end of this chapter to find out what you value most in life.

____1. To be reasonably sure about the future for myself and my family.
____2. To have influence over people.
____3. To have people think well of me.
____4. To do things for my family and others.

___

[70] Petitpas, et al., Ibid.

___5. To have as much freedom as possible to do the things I want to do.

___6. To do new and different things often.

___7. To have friends.

___8. To create an atmosphere that makes for satisfying family living.

___9. To do what is right according to my beliefs.

___10. To have things neat, orderly, and organized.

___11. To have as many good things as possible.

___12. To do things well.

CAREER EXPLORATION

Resume writing, interviewing, mentorships, internships, and working during the off-season (when possible) will help you get job experience. These opportunities will help you acquire the specific knowledge, attitudes, and skills required for employment outside of hockey. Your goal should be to translate "in hockey" success into your life "after hockey".

SOURCES OF INFORMATION FOR CAREER DEVELOPMENT

Teachers   Professionals
Internet   Job Fairs
Career Books   Job Shadowing
Career Centers/Counselors   Internships/Mentorships
Temporary Jobs

HOCKEY CREATES OPPORTUNITIES

In terms of contacts, hockey provides many opportunities. When Keith Magnuson (Chicago Blackhawks) quit hockey, he had thought carefully about his future.

Company president Bill O'Rourke helped find a position with Joyce Beverages, a Chicago-based bottler and distiller.[71] However, not all players receive help. Other players are overprotected because of their athletic skills. Some players assume that hockey management personnel will take care of them even after their careers are over. For a few franchise players, their marketability and name recognition may generate opportunities, but such advantages quickly disappear after retirement.[72] Therefore, planning becomes an essential factor in developing a post-hockey career.

CAREERS THAT ALLOW YOU TO STAY NEAR HOCKEY

Barry Melrose uses the skills he developed as a player and coach to provide insightful color commentary on ESPN and as a writer for ESPN magazine. Former athletes are a source of hockey knowledge with respect to skill, technique, strategy, and physiological and mental training. Neil Sheehy, a Harvard graduate who was a defenseman for the Calgary Flames, had a reputation for being a "goon". "I was one of the few guys who would go after Gretzky. Not fighting, but with a good check."[73] Instead of fighting on the ice, he now faces off against the general managers of teams as a NHL player agent. His law degree will soon help this career. The aggressive skills he learned on the rink have transferred into mental skills that still help him "beat" his opponent.

EDUCATION

Better-educated athletes leave their sports sooner than their less-educated peers. Perhaps knowing they have their education to fall back on, they feel prepared and more willing

---

[71] McFalone, ibid.
[72] Baillie
[73] Myers, p. 1A

to transition into life without hockey. On the other hand, Igor Larionov is scholarly, the author of several books, and as of 1999 was playing a major role on the Detroit Red Wings despite being in his 40's. By continuing with school, you will possess a wide array of options by being better educated. While playing for Toronto, center Billy Harris gradually accumulated credits during the summers and evenings at the University of Toronto toward his B.A. in Economics. "I was leaning toward teaching ...I had another profession in mind at the time, so it was very, very easy for me to actually make the decision to leave hockey."[74]

Developing your new career options provides you with many opportunities after you leave hockey. Balancing academics and hockey, selecting the right school, and learning transferable life skills are some of the things learned through education.

FINANCIAL PLANNING

Many hockey players who are financially successful possess few skills to earn a living outside of hockey. Often these players have a difficult time dealing with retirement. Some athletes are not able to manage their finances effectively either during their careers or after retirement. Fiscal responsibility was not learned. Avoid those situations and invest in your own future. Planning for the future financially (e.g., investments, savings, not spending beyond your means) will provide you with financial stability in the long-run.

SOCIAL IDENTITY AND SOCIAL SUPPORT

When hockey players' careers are over, they are no longer an integral part of the team or organization. As a consequence, the social support received while in sport may

---

[74] McFalone, p. 116

no longer be present. Due to a restricted social identity and the absence of alternative social support systems, retired players may feel isolated, lonely, and socially unfulfilled. Friends, acquaintances, and social activities revolved primarily around hockey. Expand your social identity by becoming active in your church or community, joining clubs, taking classes, or by working part-time. These activities will help you create a social support network outside of hockey.

HEALTH

Hockey players with chronic injuries and ailments due to numerous years of playing may be limited in their post-career options. They may also question their self-worth and long for their lost public esteem. Health problems associated with a poor transition from hockey are: weight gain, smoking, drinking, depression, anxiety, and substance abuse. In such cases it is important that hockey players "in transition" seek out the support services which are available to them (sport psychologists, counselors, physicians, etc.).

GOAL SETTING

Athletes who accomplish their hockey goals have an easier time adjusting to and making the decision to leave hockey. Review your answers from this chapter's (life skills) exercises. Use goal setting (already well explained in Chapter 5) to plan for life during, apart from, and after hockey. What skills would you like to learn or establish in hockey'? Set goals to achieve these skills. Set goals to learn and make time for different activities outside of hockey. Create a financial plan pre- and post-hockey by using goal setting. Remember that goals need to be specific, and your "big" goal should be broken down into small, achievable goals to work toward along the way.

Exercise 5

1. Identify your personal needs that are being met through hockey. What other ways can you fulfill those needs outside of/after hockey'?

_____

_____

_____

_____

_____

_____

2. Identify problems that may result from hockey retirement (e.g., absence of suitable employment or recreational activities). Develop and implement strategies (e.g., gathering career information, locating amateur sports alternatives) to cope with these negative consequences.

_____

_____

_____

_____

_____

_____

SUMMARY

Prepare yourself for your eventual departure from competitive hockey. Although this chapter has briefly touched on some of these topics, do not be afraid or embarrassed to find out about financial planning, job and educational opportunities; get help on finding a new career, interests, or activities; ask how others have dealt with life post-hockey; learn to use one's mental skills in all aspects of life; and learn about a physical fitness and nutritional conditioning/

maintaining program. Former athletes recommend planning for life after hockey while still competing by maintaining a balance in life (pursuing career and educational goals).

There is "life after sport". Denying the inevitable end to your hockey career will leave you unprepared which can result in life difficulties. Fred Barret (defenseman for Minnesota and Los Angeles) joined the fire department after his hockey career ended. "My work involves teamwork and, when the alarm goes off, there's that same rush I got as a player. There aren't many professions that offer this!"[75] Like Fred Barret and other athletes discussed in this chapter, you should think seriously about what you want to do after hockey. Use the "life skills" learned in hockey in your daily life and in your new roles of commentator, student, teacher, manager, lawyer, or coach - your choice! Use what hockey has taught you in the game of life! Use what this book has taught you -after all, it's entitled, "Mental Toughness Skills of Hockey and Beyond." Good luck in the beyond!

Key for Exercise 4: Personal Values Exercise

1. Security   (To be reasonably sure of the future for myself and my family)
2. Influence   (To have influence with people)
3. Recognition   (To have people think well of me)
4. Helpfulness   (To do things for my family and others)
5. Freedom   (To have as much freedom as possible to the things I want to do)
6. New Experience   (To do new and different things often)
7. Friendliness   (To have friends)
8. Family Life   (To arrange for a family atmosphere that makes for satisfying family living)
9. Religion   (To do what is right according to my beliefs)
10. Orderliness   (To have things neat, orderly and

---

[75] McFalone, p. 25

organized)

11. Wealth   (To have as many good things as possible)

12. Workmanship   (To do things well)

22

GOALTENDERS

"More Than Half the Team." - *Tarasov*

THE NEED FOR A HOT GOAL TENDER

Tarasov's statement of "Goaltenders: More than half the team" has come into the spotlight increasingly in the past five years, with 1994 being billed as the "year of the goaltender". Coaches, players, and general managers tend to look to "which team has a hot goalie" before they make predictions about the outcome of a championship series, such as the Stanley Cup. *Sports Illustrated* did an article during the 1994 season on the NHL's hottest goaltenders as a prelude to which teams could expect to be in the playoffs. This focus has continued into 2000.

Although goaltending has always been important, the present parity between teams has led hockey experts to believe that on any given night, the team with a "hot goaltender" will win! Those making such predictions based on goaltending were not disappointed when Mike Richter set a record for NHL playoff shutouts and Kirk McLean was in goal for the Canucks during a number of overtime wins! Patrick Roy returned from a hospital stay to stop more than 60 pucks in a single playoff game for Montreal. Dominique Hasek allowed practically no goals in the 1998 Olympics. In these years of fickle media coverage, publicity hype, and marketing of teams, a goalie may interpret such statements as either a "vote of confidence" or as unbelievable pressure. To illustrate the fickleness players experience from the media, one particular article about the 1994 Stanley Cup final series stated that all that stood between Vancouver and annihilation was the goaltending of Kirk McLean who dazzled and thwarted the

New York Rangers in Game 1, stopping 52 of their 54 shots. The same article went on to say that McLean couldn't stop a hippity-hop in Game 2 and that he totally disintegrated in Game 3.

The importance of top goaltending was also underscored in 1993 when 21 sudden death overtimes were played in the first 2 rounds of the Stanley Cup playoffs, breaking a previously held record of 16, which was set in 1982 for the entire post-season. When the New York Islanders defeated the Pittsburgh Penguins, one of the lowest paid goalies in the NHL, 30 year old Glenn Healey, completely outplayed his Pittsburgh counterpart, Vezina candidate, Tom Barrasso. It was said that mid-series, Barrasso began giving away "more softies than a Dairy Queen". Conversely, when Jacque Demers was coaching Montreal, he felt so secure with Patrick Roy in the net that he opened up the game to let his offensive-minded players play their game, a decision that led to a 1993 Stanley Cup. Ed Belfour came through the 1999 Stanley Cup with solid goaltending for the Dallas Stars. His solid play gave his teammates confidence.

PRESSURE ON GOALTENDERS

Well, how do goalies, or put another way, how can one man or woman shoulder the responsibility of being "more than half a team""? Clearly, there is a great deal of stress experienced by many goalies. These stresses emanate from a fear of failure associated with concerns about: (1) fear of losing; (2) fear of letting your coach, team, self, and significant others down; (3) fear of being replaced in the net; (4) fear of giving up goals and being embarrassed; and (5) in a strange way, fear of being hurt, injured, or in pain.

When these or other stresses are experienced over a number of seasons, they may accumulate, often with tragic results. According to Gordie & Colleen Howes' book, *After the Applause,* goalies Gump Worsley acknowledged he had suffered a nervous breakdown while playing goal for the Montreal Canadians, Terry Sawchuck suffered from intense nervous disorders, and Glenn Hall routinely vomited between periods. Ken Dryden, who played in goal for the Montreal Canadians (much of the time under Coach Scotty Bowman) for six Stanley Cup victories, describes some of the fears he experienced, "When I see a player draw back his stick to shoot, when my concentration must turn to commitment, my body stiffens, my eyes widen and go sightless, my head lifts in the air, and I bail out as if leaving an empty body to cover the net." While Dryden may have exaggerated, students of the game have all observed a "psyched out" goalie on occasion.

Ron Hextall the goaltender who has scored goals, speaks of his first game in the NHL when he started for Philadelphia against the Edmonton Oilers, "I didn't pay much attention to the crowd or fans because I was concentrating so much on the game. I was extremely nervous! Who wouldn't be. And when I saw Gretzky skating around, I told myself, 'Just play hard, that's all that you can do'." Although goalies such as Felix Potvin of Toronto and Patrick Roy of Montreal are said to have 'nerves of steel' and have received rave reviews for their consistency, only they know to what degree they may have internally experienced the negative effects of sustained pressure.

Goalies at other levels of play such as minor league championships with their tie-breaking overtimes and shootouts, the Olympics, World Tournaments, World Junior Championships, NCAA, USHL, the Minnesota State High School Tournament, and Bantam Tournaments are all at levels of participation which attract fans, media scrutiny, and a critique of the game.

Goaltending determined the 1988 Olympics and the 1994 Olympics was won in a shootout when Sweden defeated Canada. In the 1994 World Tournament, Canada emerged the winner defeating Sweden in a shootout! Quite the situations for goalies to be in! A game of inches with national pride on the line!

THE GOALIE MYSTIQUE

Despite the obvious importance of goaltending in hockey, little is really known about how goalies prepare for games, what they like to think about, and how they like to be feeling when in the net. To date, we have only the accounts of players such as Ken Dryden, Ken Bertanga, Tony Esposito, Tretiak, and a handful of others who fortunately have shared some insights into their pre-game preparation. For the most part, coaches, players, and sport scientists do not understand the goalie mystique. Because of this, the AHAUS Goalkeeping book states that <u>coaches</u> <u>feel most helpless in dealing with goalies and the mental part of goalkeeping.</u> Players and coaches remain fearful of rocking the boat when a goaltender is on a hot streak and are prompted to leave the goaltender alone to 'slumpbust' when he's not.

Many goalies I have worked with, when left on their own to get themselves mentally prepared, have sought help from sources such as transcendental meditation, gurus, some paralyzing superstitions, hypnosis, and habits such as staring into black corners to enlarge their pupils. How can a coach help? One thing is certain, goaltenders must not be denied the same opportunity to learn mental skills that are available to other players. If the team becomes afraid of breaking a goaltender's hot streak, then the team is sending the message to the goalie that his performance is externally controlled. That insinuates that the goalie is influenced more by luck than by the ability and effort he puts into his performance.

Fortunately, to date, a few persons knowledgeable about the mental demands of goaltending have provided some assistance. The AHAUS Coaches Goalkeeping Handbook by Blase, Peterson, and Bertanga (1985) contains an excellent chapter on "The Mental Game" as does Joe Bertanga's book on Goaltending(1990). Keith Allain, assistant coach for the 1992 US Olympic Team, also has a booklet "Goaltending: The Mental Game".

Mental preparation that might be helpful for goaltenders before their games should not be very different from the format used by forwards, defensemen, and athletes in other sports. Mental preparation should not take more than 45 minutes and ideally, as explained elsewhere in this book, it should be a combination of a mental preparation plan, goal setting, positive self talk, re-focusing strategies, relaxation as necessary, and mental imagery.

Goaltenders can briefly read over their mental preparation plans, write down their goals for the game, do their relaxation technique, and "image" themselves dressed in their uniforms, on the ice, in the net, in the appropriate arena, with the fans, crowd noise, and opposing team. Goalies should see themselves poised, anticipating, feeling ready, and making the saves they expect to make. This period of mental rehearsal provides them with an opportunity to "be all there" in their mind's eye. They can see themselves performing consistently, confidently, maintaining their concentration, and anticipating (reading and reacting) to plays before they develop. They see themselves looking the part of a confident goalie: good posture with crisp, precise passing, handling rebounds well, and making saves.

The four mental foci of consistency, concentration, anticipation, and confidence are highlighted.[76] Although

---

[76] Blase, Peterson & Bertanga

these are covered elsewhere in *Power Play,* we shall briefly paraphrase some of the important points, and refer interested readers to the reference list for additional information on goaltending. Bertanga (1990) stresses that goalies need to love the game, be confident, be under emotional control, and be able to objectively and maturely evaluate one's performance, make adjustments when indicated, and maintain a sense of humor.

CONSISTENCY

Goalies must play all shots the same, no matter what the circumstances. Goaltenders must consistently follow each shot, no matter who takes it, where it is shot from, what the score is, or in spite of how much time is left in the game. The goalie's task is to be able to "channel click" (see chapter 10) to the present- to the now, to be all in the moment. Evaluation must wait until between periods or after the game. Image how you want to see yourself in the net.

In addition to using the channel clicking technique to stay in the "now", it is also used to stay on the positive channel. Being positive means striving to maintain an aggressive, fighting to win, invincible, courageous attitude, and demeanor. This must apply to both physical and mental responses. To do this, goalies must remain cool, alert, focused, and precise, handling the puck at all times crisply and with assurance! Goalies want to play pumped, yet relaxed, so muscles are quick and responsive. In other words "ride the horse in the direction that it's going" to get the best performance and avoid fighting the puck.[77]

To be a consistent goaltender such as is said of Patrick Roy, Mike Richter, and Curtis Joseph every situation, player, and team must be responded to with equal effort. Bertanga suggests that the mind be rested when face-offs are at the other

[77] Wall & Russell (1992)

end and between periods. But the rest of the time, the goalie needs to concentrate.

CONFIDENCE

Some authors believe that a goalie's confidence changes within a season, a tournament, or a game. I can usually see immediately (shot-by-shot) when confidence is lost or gained by a goalie's change in posture, eye contact, handling of the puck, etc. Many coaches and scouts see it much faster than I do. It's the same way I can see when patients are stressed, frightened, or lacking confidence. In my office, it's the temperature and texture of the handshake, the eye contact, the facial expression, voice level, etc. On the ice, it's the set of the goalie's shoulders, the carriage of the body, the flourish of the skills, the crispness in handling rebounds, reading plays, the astuteness of the anticipation, and the correctness of the body positioning.

When A Goal Is Scored On A Goalie

Bertanga suggests that when a goalie is scored on, he skate forward actively to the edge of the crease to symbolically clear his head and then re-enter the net, refocused. Any gesture that is done consistently can be paired with a mental response. For example, taking two strides forward and "clearing the front of the net with the stick" might be paired with a "clearing" of the mind. Clearing thoughts of "how and why" he or she was scored on is imperative.

Some goaltenders have told me that goalie coaches who are most helpful have been able to come into the locker room between periods and without disturbing the rest of the team, have made one or two constructive, helpful comments pertaining to their physical or psychological behavior during the previous period. My sense is that goalies do not wish to be embarrassed or have their teammates distracted. Yet, carefully thought-out correction can be well received. After the game, goalies can evaluate and analyze the good and bad aspects of their on-ice performances so they can reinforce what was good and make corrections to eliminate errors.

ANTICIPATION

Anticipation, according to Tarasov, is the goalie's ability to anticipate events, to predict the opponent's move, to react before the play develops, yet to have patience. I used to believe that uptight players, under the influence of too much adrenaline, were unable to see the whole ice, or all the options, because of tunnel vision. While that may be partially true, I've since learned that peripheral vision is less affected than I thought, but instead, it's the brain's inability to react to the play correctly when the goalie is under stress that causes the problem. Because anticipation is so important, goalies must become proficient at using psychological skills training (PST) such as relaxation to help them attain their ideal performance state (calm but pumped). Because anticipation is closely aligned to the reading of visual cues, it is particularly important that goaltenders be psyched right. Salmela (1970), a researcher, found that visual information (more cues available for the wrist shot than the slap shot) that facilitates anticipation is available and useable during the pre-shot period. (See the section on Research on Goaltending for an elaboration of what "psyched right" means for many goalies.)

SPECIFICS FOR GOALTENDING

Goaltenders occupy a unique position on the ice and encounter different concentration problems than their teammates. The following is a short list of tips specific to goaltenders that might be helpful:

1. Practice concentrating for progressively longer periods of time.

2. Goaltenders in the NHL have the challenge of staying associated (focused) and concentrating for long periods of time. Because the number of shots on net increases dramatically, as does the speed of the shooter's release, turnovers, and breakaways, goalies are forced to keep their heads in the game for longer periods.

3. Practice sessions for goaltenders using relaxation and focusing on their breathing must simulate actual game conditions. Therefore, relaxation and imagery drills should train the goalie to focus on making save after save with all senses involved for the length of time that game conditions might require.

4. Goalies can use line changes, penalties, and face-offs (at the other end) to take a quick physical and mental break. This is the time to stand up straight, stretch, let the mind wander briefly, and then refocus on the 'now'.

5. Many goaltenders actively maintain concentration by staying physically and/or verbally involved in the game. Even if there is not much action at their end, some have rituals of banging the goal pipes, talking to the referees, teammates, or opponents. There are any number of activities to help them stay engaged in the game. These interactions help some goalies remain alert, focused, proactive, and reactive.

CONCENTRATION

All goaltenders are concerned about concentration. Ken Dryden played before the days of sport psychology and the availability of personalized audiocassettes or videotapes that have relaxation and the positive imagery of hockey skills on them. However, Dryden used to make a ritual of the whole day of a game, which extended right through to his dressing routine. He dressed at a steady, preoccupying pace: at 7:07 he donned his pants, by 7:12 skates, by 7:17 pads, by 7:20 vest and sweater. Dryden had this to say about his ritual and mental preparation, "Too fast and with nothing to do, I think about the game or whatever else comes into my mind, too slow, and I rush and by rushing I wonder if I've somehow affected how I will play. Not wanting to think about the game or something other than the game, I keep rigidly on a schedule. I want to arrive at game time, undistracted, my mind blank, my emotions under control. If I can do that, the rest of me is ready."[78] Now, goalies have audiocassettes and videotapes such as "Hot Goaltending", which help promote the confidence, relaxation, concentration, consistency, and anticipation posited by Peterson and Bertanga as important.

Goaltending schools and USA Hockey Goalie Camps expose goalies to the expertise offered by those who truly understand and can demonstrate the art of goaltending. Goalie camps and goaltending schools deliberately design exercises to simulate game conditions rather than challenging goalies with what Bertanga (1990) describes as the "guilt and volume" routines too often ordered by non-goaltending coaches. Although some improvements have been made in the past decade to help goaltenders execute the tasks required of them, little basic sports science research has been done on the physical and psychological demands of this important sport position. What little research has been done, thus far, has focused on physical parameters such as % B.F., height, weight, VO_2, max, target heart rate, and anaerobic power.

I have worked with goaltenders the past 7-8 years

---

[78] Dryden, K. Ibid. p. 171

who ranged from being the most fit athlete on their team, to those who were unable to see because of no glasses, to others who arrived in USHL Junior hockey well versed in sport psychology with their own performance enhancement tapes. Some goalies prepared for competition by staring into a black corner to dilate their pupils, believing they were increasing visual acuity. Others are cosmic or meditational in their mental preparation. Still, others seem similar to ski racer Picabo Street, who feels most competent when feverishly wound up, favoring performing out on the edge, totally psyched up!

YEARS OF RESEARCH ON HOCKEY GOALTENDERS

Because of the diversity in the anecdotal accounts of the mental preparation of goalies and the strategies used to stay focused, we decided to sample large numbers of goalies to see if we could establish averages for the mind and body experience (physical and psychological variables) experienced during on-ice performances.

Research Phase I

During the 1993 season we initiated a long term research program on ice hockey goalies. We began by asking 69 youth goaltenders between the ages of 10-18 whether the mental or physical aspects of goaltending were the most difficult. The majority (76%) said the mental aspects of the game were most difficult. Clearly, those goalies were hungry for assistance and it was clear they needed to be included in all team mental toughness exercises and discussions. Just as important was our realization that neither goalies, coaches, nor sport psychologists were sure how to help goalies reduce their stress and cope with the mental demands of their position.

We then asked the same 69 goalies their reasons for becoming goaltenders. Their answers ranged from "it's actually a spiritual position", "you get to play the whole game", "I traded with my friend", "my Dad suggested it", "you get to look fancy in your pads", to "I didn't know what offsides were".

Research Phase 2

The next stage of our research was a multidisciplinary study in which sport anxiety tests, heart rate (HR) telemetry, skin temperature tests, videotapes from goalies in net at a puck shooting station (PSM) and an immediate recall post-session were evaluated on 42 goalies to gain a better understanding of the physical and psychological demands of goaltending. At the PSM skill station, HR ranged between 112-208. HR at stations other than the PSM, such as the "breakaway" station ranged between 128-208 bpm and average HR was 173 bpm. In a paper published in the Mayo Clinic Proceedings in 1998, we reported that goalies who performed best had faster HR's, were older, more experienced, lower in somatic anxiety (awareness of body tension), and higher in confidence.

Research Phase 3

In Phase 3 of the goalie research, we examined 13 goalies during one, two, or three league games to understand at what level of arousal (or the zone of optimal functioning [ZOF] goalies perform best. Goalies completed the same anxiety tests prior to their games and wore HR telemetry units in a little pack at the back around their waists (Figure 1).

The HR (ECG signal) was superimposed with the videotape of the goalie's performance. Although 26 games of complete data on 13 goalies showed the average HR was 150 bpm, there were some goalies whose HR's were much faster. One high school goalie had 92%, 96%, and 100% saves during which time his average game HR's were 164, 173, and

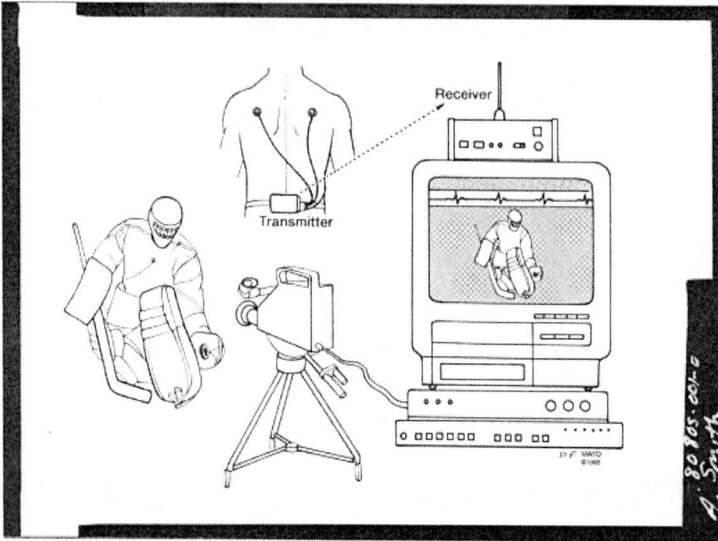

178 bpm for the same three games. Notice (in Figure 2) the shutout occurred when his average HR for the game was 178 bpm. His trait and state levels of anxiety were very average. Trait anxiety is the predisposition a person has to view events as threatening, a characteristic that is usually unchanged. State anxiety measures the amount of tension a person is experiencing in a specific situation (e.g., in a breakaway or in a big playoff game). This goalie played extremely well at a high level of arousal.

One goalie who later played Division I hockey may have had a similar ZOF, as the plan (determined by his coach

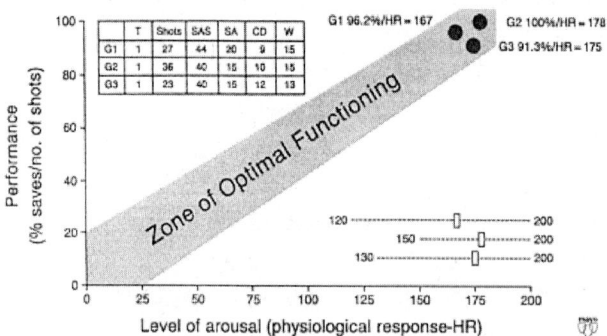

	T	Shots	SAS	SA	CD	W
G1	1	27	44	20	9	15
G2	1	36	40	15	10	15
G3	1	23	40	15	12	13

G1 96.2%/HR = 167
G2 100%/HR = 178
G3 91.3%/HR = 175

Zone of Optimal Functioning

Performance (% saves/no. of shots)

Level of arousal (physiological response-HR)

and I) for the high school state tournament was to have his teammates frequently skate by to interact with him, bang his pads, etc. He clearly played best when he was emotionally up, on the balls of his skates, interacting, and reacting. When Karl Goehring (who was later the goalie for the North Dakota Fighting Sioux) played for Apple Valley in the Minnesota High School State Hockey Tournament, the game was won at 2 a.m., after five overtime periods. Knowing that goalies experience fast HR's during games prompted us to assess the effect of prolonged arousal on the body.

Research Phase 4

In Phase 4 of the goalie research, our sports medicine team attended a goalie camp and measured 20 goalies in the morning and in the afternoon as they rotated through on-ice stations. In addition to HR, we measured salivary cortisol (a hormone that increases in the saliva in response to stress), anxiety, mood state, and confidence. Twelve goalies were classified as non-responders and eight were classified as responders. This indicated that eight of the 20 goalies increased their salivary cortisol levels quite markedly in contrast to the other goalies. Even within the eight responders, there were very different skill stations for each goalie that caused stress.

Research Phase 5

In our most recent study, 10 goalies were studied in high school and United States Hockey League (USHL) games to examine the same variables in relation to performance. Although average game HR's were 150 bpm and ranged between 130-161 bpm, not as high as in a previous study, maximum HR again ranged between 180-220 bpm. Average salivary cortisol levels (SCL) almost doubled between pre-game and after the first and second periods. For one goalie, mean HR for one game was 167 bpm, and during one period HR averaged 174 bpm. The goalie faced 16 shots that period and saved 15 (91.7%). After that period, SCL was 8 times higher than baseline. His % saves for his three games were 89%, 90%, and 91 %. Although performance may not be affected by the physiological response, the emotional cost of playing goaltender may be much higher for one goalie than for another.

We have learned much about hockey goalies. We still need to know how best to condition goalies so they can function with the high adrenaline level that occurs in response to the excitement of playing goal. Because we are able to synchronize HR with the videotape, it is clear from our studies that often the fast HR (catecholamine response) simply occurs secondary to anticipation when the goaltender is standing still, seeing a breakaway or a 3 on 1 coming down the ice. The adrenaline rush is probably necessary for the quick eye-to-hand or eye-to-foot reaction time needed to make the big save!

In conclusion, goalies should be exposed to sport psychology in hopes that psychological skills training (PST) strategies shown to be effective with other athletes will be helpful for them. Furthermore, if the goalie mentally prepares using strategies such as relaxation, goal setting, and imagery, which are understood by the coach, then, when problems do arise, the coach and the goalie are able to communicate and understand each other. Together they will be more likely to find workable solutions. Otherwise, as the pressures to succeed increase, goalies will be forced to find alternative coping strategies, such as the list of superstitions, Dryden felt too embarrassed to talk about or other less healthy methods. These less healthy ways of handling stress widen the gap that may already exist between a coach and his or her very important player.

The ritual that players like Dryden followed "ate up" the whole day. Fortunately, now with an individualized mental preparation plans, such as what we are describing in *Power Play,* goaltenders can adequately prepare for a game in less than an hour and feel confident. This increases their sense of control, allows for more meaningful interaction with their families and teammates, and hopefully eliminates a need for "camping out over the toilet". The following script is representative of those we write after interviewing the goalie, review with the goalie, and then record on an audiotape. Goalies can listen to these positive imagery scripts prior to their games so they take to the ice "calm but pumped" and ready to go! The imagery portion of this script is proceeded by the adapted relaxation method taught in chapter 8.

Now that I am feeling really relaxed, I let my mind go to hockey. I realize I am growing a lot this year. I have started to see that my goalie coach has made some suggestions that I can benefit from. I am starting to trust him as I know he watches me consistently and can see what I need to change. I've tried to stop resisting him and his suggestions and let the good ones be received. I'm trying to be coachable. I've also learned that I need to play all games, one puck at a time, one shot at a time, regardless of who fires them. I need to get pumped for every game and know that on any day, in any game, I can stop anyone in the league. I don't care this year who I play, what color their uniforms are, or how good the shooters are. I simply play my game, my position. I keep my eye on the puck. I make each stop. I play my angle. I see myself "in the zone", looking strong, confident, cat-like, and agile. I've learned to be more mentally tough. I don't let a certain team or shooter control me or my thoughts. I am the man. I believe in me, in my team, in my head coach, and in his coaching staff. I know each shot comes to me free of a past, it's an event, independent. If I can see it, I can stop it. I feel balanced on my skates. My glove and blocker feel quick and sure.

My feet are just waiting for quick saves. Furthermore, I am so into the game that I'm not aware of myself. I don't feel shy and I don't feel like a show-off. I just quietly feel pumped and I feel good. My only thought is to be where the puck is. Each game, I prepare the same way. Each stop I make. I don't let myself emotionally get too high or too low. I just know it's my job, it's what I do. I feel focused, strong, bold, but cool, like an ice man, like a champion. I feel invincible. No one can get to me because I am in my zone. I know I am good and the zone is mine. I control it. I don't get down and I battle every puck. It's a war zone and the cage is mine to defend. I love this game, and I love being a great goalie!

HUMOR AND ATTITUDE

When Don Beaupre was challenged by reports about his size with the inference that he was 'too small' to be a net minder, he quipped his response, "I only have to stop the puck, I don't have to kill it." Daryl Sittler wrote that when Mike Palmiteer played goaltender for the Toronto Maple Leafs, "What got us believing in him was his attitude. He treated every goal against him like it was a fluke! He could get you pumped up and the crowd behind him." Most importantly, goalies must simply put a positive spin on who they are. If you are naturally quiet and focused, then maximize those attributes by conveying confidence and focus to your teammates. If you, honestly, are a Palmiteer and play with attitude, then exude confidence and bravado. To thine own self be true. Regardless of "who you are" as a person and as a goalie, remain humble enough to be coachable. As knowledge of the art and science of goaltending grows, so must you!

"If I can see it, I can stop it."

In conclusion, it is hoped that <u>Power Play</u> has provided worthwhile information that will assist players, coaches, and parents to gain a better understanding of the concepts and strategies to improve Mental Toughness, and as a result, increase the player's enjoyment of the game. For above all, we must remember, it is a game and no matter the stakes, it must be played competitively, fairly, and most importantly, for FUN. Wherever possible, and to the best of my knowledge, credit has been given to the appropriate sources for ideas or material implemented into <u>Power Play</u>. Please write us with any comments, criticisms, or suggestions that we can use to improve the next edition. Thanks for your support.

Do you wonder why we love them?

Well, neither do I.

Most players I know are fine young men
ON and OFF THE ICE.

Cheers

REFERENCES

Anderson, Bob		Stretching
Anderson, Kelli	(1999)	Sports Illustrated
Baillie, P.H.	(1993)	Understanding Retirement from Sports: Therapeutic Ideas for HelpingAthletes in Transition
Benson, Herbert	(1976)	The Relaxation Response
Blatherwick, Jack	(1991)	Over Speed: Skill Training for Hockey
Brewer, B.; Van Raalte, J.; and Linder, D.	(1993)	Athletic Identity: Hercules' Muscles or Achilles Heel?
Chartrand, J. and Lent, R.	(1987)	Sports Counseling: Enhancing the Development of the Student-Athlete
Clark, Nancy R.D.MS		Traveling Tips for Athletes
Davis, Hap.		Perceptual & Motor Skills
Davis, James	(1988)	Strategies for Managing Athletes' Jet Lag
Dryden, Ken	(1983)	The Game
Dortinan, H.A. & Kuchl, Karl	(1991)	The Mental Game of Baseball: A Guide to PeakPerformance
Fischler, Stan	(1990)	Golden Ice
Gould, Daniel and Horn, Thelma	(1984)	Participation Motivation in Young Athletes

Gould, Daniel;
Petlichkoff, Linda;
Hodge, Kenneth and
Simons, Jeffery   (1990)   Evaluating the
                                     Effectiveness of a
                                     Psychological Skills
                                     Educational Workshop
Greer, Nancy Dr.   Personal
                                     Communication
Gretzky, Wayne   (1990)   Gretzky, An
                                     Autobiography
Halliwell, Wayne   (1988)   Video of Ron Hextall
                                     "psyching up"to In
                                     The Heat Of The
                                     Night, CASSMontreal,
                                     Quebec.

Harris, Dorothy &
Harris, Bette   (1984)   The Athlete's Guide
                                     to Sport Psychology:
                                     Mental Skills For
                                     Physical People

Howe, C.; Howe, G.; and
Wilkins, C.   (1990)   After the Applause
Irvin, D.   (1992)   The HABS
Jarvis, Doug   Hockey Magazine
Kaufman, Mark   (1990)   Ideas for goal setting for
                                     hockey players
Lewallen, Jack Dr.   (1986)   Anecdote shared at
                                     a hockey Seminar in
                                     Minneapolis
Loehr, James   (1982)   Mental Toughness
Martens, Ranier   (1987)   Coaching Psychology
Miller, Merry Dr.   Sport Confidence. Sport
                                     Psychology Training
                                     Bulletin

New Games
Ogilvie, Bruce   Tape "What Price
                                     Glory'?" CBS

Orlick, Terry	(1986)	Psyching for Sport: Mental Training for Athletes
Orlick, Terry; Ravizza,Ken; and Rotella, Bob	(1989)	CASS, Montreal
Salming, B.; and Karlsson, G.	(1991)	Blood, Sweat, and Hockey
Smith, Aynsley	(1986)	Adapted Relaxation Method
Smith, Aynsley	(1990)	The Emotional Responses of Athletes to Injury. Mayo Clinic Proceeding
Smith, Michael D.	(1988)	Sources of Violence in Ice Hockey
Stuart, M.J.; Smith, A.M.; and Kaufman, M.	(1995)	Injuries in Junior A Ice Hockey: A Three-Year Prospective Study
Suinn, Richard		Visual Motor Behavioral Rehearsal
Sutherland G. W.	(1976)	Fire on Ice
Taylor, J.; and Olgivie, B.	(1994)	A Conceptual Model of Adaptation to Retirement Among Athletes
Thorton, Jim	(1993)	Special Report: Kids in Sport
Toronto Maple Leafs Official Game Magazine	(1994)	Hockey Night in Toronto
Wong, G.	(1996)	A Hockey Kind of Guy